Next Level Basic

Next Level Basic

THE DEFINITIVE
BASIC BITCH HANDBOOK

STASSI SCHROEDER

G

GALLERY BOOKS

New York London Toronto Sydney New Delhi

Gallery Books
An Imprint of Simon & Schuster, Inc.
1230 Avenue of the Americas
New York, NY 10020

First Gallery Books hardcover edition April 2019

GALLERY BOOKS and colophon are registered trademarks of Simon & Schuster, Inc.

For information about special discounts for bulk purchases, please contact Simon & Schuster Special Sales at 1-866-506-1949 or business@simonandschuster.com.

The Simon & Schuster Speakers Bureau can bring authors to your live event. For more information or to book an event, contact the Simon & Schuster Speakers Bureau at 1-866-248-3049 or visit our website at www.simonspeakers.com.

Interior design by Jaime Putorti
Illustrations by Hannah M. Brown

Manufactured in the United States of America

10 9 8 7 6

Library of Congress Cataloging-in-Publication Data

Names: Schroeder, Stassi, author.
Title: Next level basic : the definitive basic bitch handbook / Stassi Schroeder.
Description: First Gallery Books hardcover edition. | New York, NY : Gallery Books, 2019.
Identifiers: LCCN 2018060279 (print) | LCCN 2019010689 (ebook) |
    ISBN 9781982112486 (ebook) | ISBN 9781982112462 (hardcover : alk. paper)
Subjects: LCSH: Self-acceptance—Humor.
Classification: LCC BF575.S37 (ebook) | LCC BF575.S37 S37 2019 (print) |
    DDC 158.1—dc23
LC record available at https://urldefense.proofpoint.com/v2/url?u=https-3A__lccn
.loc.gov_2018060279&d=DwIFAg&c=jGUuvAdBXp_VqQ6t0yah2g&r=7Powwey
p97H7BrdRqAm-eJjycEUd2REgi140E_-eJsoFHotHpuSHVST6CEgk6PFC&m=u
mvqqF30W-UlftQnj5njDN9I3AEFgGKK-yUToPBdfu0&s=V9GYm8OfoTGCf
Cb_OSw3Zr1qb_7jksCP9oHNzziZTMs&e=

ISBN 978-1-9821-1246-2
ISBN 978-1-9821-1248-6 (ebook)

For Beau—

thank you for encouraging me to own

my basic bitch every single day.

Contents

CONTENTS

Section III Hot AF

Section IV Eat, Drink, and Be Enlightened AF

Introduction

First let me say, despite what you might think if you've seen me on *Vanderpump Rules*—I am not an authority on life what-so-fucking-ever. But I am a *premiere* authority on being basic AF. I'm opinionated and judgy (which is one of my main skills, and if they gave out Academy Awards for judginess I would definitely need a trophy room), so I have some pretty strong opinions about what's important in life: ranch dressing, ghost tours, cocktails, hangover patches, hot dogs, actual dogs, the perfect pair of Loubs, *Game of Thrones*, and Ouija boards, to name a few things.

In my experience, there's nothing more boring than people who take themselves way too seriously (I live in LA, so I should know). This book is for everyone out there who is tired of pretending they would rather read *War and Peace* or see a Daniel Day-Lewis movie about *sewing* than watch a *Saw* marathon and drink a delicious but basic AF cocktail like a Kir Royale (nine parts champagne and one part crème de cassis, whatever that is. The point is, it's mainly champagne). This book is for people who want to let their basicness shine and listen to show tunes while they drive to the gym (with a full face of makeup, natch), but then drive past the gym and head to the bar instead. It's for the Khaleesis* of the world, who know that the best way to get over a breakup is to assert your authority and coerce people into doing things for you (in 2019 that means having them buy you pizza and wine), and express your rage by any means necessary (in my case, that means singing show tunes at the top of my lungs). I've survived some very public and dramatic breakups, often with a camera crew documenting the entire before and after, so you could say that getting through them is one of my specialties.

So, no, I'm not ever going to be featured on Goop or give a TED Talk, but I do know some things. Like, let's be real—everyone wants to look good AF on Instagram, and I can help with that. Most people would secretly rather eat the best hot dog on the planet than eat $26 roasted heirloom baby kumquats with a foam framboise reduction (and I can help with that too!). All

---

* Since starting my podcast, a community of *badass*, smart, funny basic bitches has organically arisen. And those BABBs are called Khaleesis. I mean, it's pretty basic to name Khaleesi as your fave *Game of Thrones* character, because she is kind of the ancient version of a basic bitch, with her platinum-blond hair and braids. So it only makes sense that fans of my podcast are named after her. . . .

humans have basic tendencies, and I am the living embodiment of a human who embraces her inner basic bitch, with pride.

In this book, I'm not going to share deep life lessons about finding myself during an (expensive) ayahuasca ceremony in the Amazon or feel-good stories that make it seem like I have it all figured out. This is me getting real, raw, and taking my basicness (and hopefully yours) to the next level, because embracing those tendencies can give you the confidence to speak up and do things you might never attempt if you were hiding your truest, most basic self. Reading this book will be like catching up with your honest, and yes, slightly bitchy friend. I *will* tell stories about losing my virginity, totally screwing up on social media, and learning that I don't know shit about life—which is a pretty good lesson to learn in your twenties—and how not everything can be solved by bingeing on Taco Bell. I'll explain what *not* to do on Instagram or Twitter (like, everyone knows that picture of you "sleeping" is really a selfie). I'll tell stories about being basic AF in high school, and then basic AF in my twenties, and I'll reveal embarrassing and true moments from my life (because not *everything* ends up on *Vanderpump*!) that prove that being basic 2.0 takes guts. I mean, you have to be kind of brave to live in foodie LA and admit that hot dogs and Cool Ranch Doritos are among your favorite foods. But YOLO, right?

I hope you can read this book and not only have a laugh and a little departure from the stresses of your everyday life but also feel like you can relate. We need to take back the joy of being basic and wear it as a badge of honor. The next time you go on a first date or meet a new group of people, I hope you feel comfortable being exactly who you are and that you don't worry about saying or doing the "right" thing, because there is no "right" thing. Except when it comes to charging your cell phone. People who run out of charge are the worst and they deserve to be slowly tortured with nipple clamps, and with this book I am going to prove it!

If you're not yet basic AF, I'm not judging you. Well, maybe I'm judging you a little. What I want is for everyone to embrace whatever they're into, even if society or their boss or some asshole online says it's lame. If you think chanting in a yoga class is the best thing ever, then good for you (even though it makes me want to gouge my eyes out with steaming-hot pokers). If you want to order the seasonal sugar-filled pumpkin-flavored whatever at Starbucks rather than some froufrou European drink, own your truth. Embracing your basicness can actually make you a happier person for one simple reason—because it's *fun*. It's so much more fulfilling to bond with people over your shared love of, say, overplayed pop songs or astrology than it is to sit in a corner and act like a hater. It gives you a sense of community and bonds you with strangers in a world that can be pretty isolating and harsh. It's a lot more fulfilling to sing "Sweet Caroline" in a bar with a bunch of strangers than it is to pretend that you don't know the words, missing out on something that's fun, memorable (depending on how many shots you do), and social. That's the essence of the Next Level Basic mentality—stop being a hater and enjoy yourself!

If your perfect day means a *Kardashian* marathon on the couch with an Aperol Spritz, that doesn't make you any less cool than the guy who spends his day home with his microbrew, listening to jazz (which sounds boring AF, BTW). Personally, I'm tired of people feeling ashamed of what they're into just because they're afraid someone might make fun of their love of bedazzled ranch dressing bottles or because they watched Kylie's ten-minute pregnancy video more than once. I mean, I did. And if you didn't, I bet you're tempted to google it right this second. Welcome to Next Level Basic.

Maybe you totally believe in the whole Mercury-in-retrograde thing (I do). Maybe you idolize Chrissy Teigen (who doesn't?). And maybe you really love the whole rosé-in-a-can craze. So what if someone else says pink wine in a can is lame? Life is way too short to care what someone else thinks about what *you* think is cool, especially when it comes to something as personal as wine. So let's stop taking ourselves so seriously and get back to basic—because I bet even Dame Judi Dench is probably out there at the local pub living her Next Level Basic best life. Let's follow her lead.

SECTION I

CHAPTER 1

Find Your Voice

You might not be shocked to find out that I was never a wallflower, but I was also not a "typical" teenager. I mean, sure, I hung out at malls and got embarrassed by my parents if they were anywhere near me in a public place, but I also pretended to read tarot cards and practiced mental telepathy, which (*shocker*) never really worked out. So I guess you could say I was *quirky*. In grammar school in New Orleans, I was the student council president because I ran a pretty kick-ass campaign where I plastered every wall of the school with posters that had a cartoon version of my face on them, plus streamers and glitter (looking back, it was a precursor to my current passion for party planning). Had Instagram been around back then, I would have paid the people in my school with the most followers to do sponsored posts for me.

Was this basic? It definitely was. But I still had a lot to learn. The thing is—taking your basicness to the next level is a process. It takes confidence, y'all. We all have basic tendencies, but *admitting* those tendencies like a boss bitch is the key. Embracing your most basic self and not caring what anyone says about your love of selfies or your passion for *My 600-lb Life* means you have become a confident badass who speaks her mind and doesn't care what the trolls have to say about it. What I'm saying is: to be a Next Level Basic bitch, you first have to be a boss bitch. I learned this lesson pretty early on.

I've been called "Bossy Stassi" for as long as I can remember—and I take that nickname as a compliment. The teachers at school once called my mom and dad to tell them that other parents were complaining because their kids weren't getting enough attention—because I was stealing it all by being a kiss-ass who loved to ham it up. I was the quintessential hand raiser in class, so being the center of attention has just always been standard for me. I legit can't help it. (God, I'm such a freaking asshole.) You might say I was born to be a reality-show whore and share everything about my life with anyone who will watch. It's just my destiny. BTW, I'm aware of how ridiculous it sounds to say that reality TV is my destiny when people in history like Gandhi and Mother Teresa actually got real shit done, but reality TV just feels like something I was meant to do—for the greater good of humanity. (Just kidding!)

So holla if you, like me, always felt you were special. Like you just looked around and knew you were different. And it's not because you were smarter than anyone, or *cooler* than anyone, but because you just had something that's a little different and unique. And I'll just add—why is it considered a douchey thing to say that you're special? Do you think Beyoncé is ashamed of being special? Exactly. We should all feel freaking special, even if we're not dancing *and* singing on a giant stage in six-inch stiletto thigh-high boots, as pillars of fire shoot up all around us and millions of people watch our every move. You're special. So don't apologize for it—embrace it!

A long time ago I realized that strong, opinionated, comfortable-in-their-own-skin *bawse queens* are often labeled "bitches." And you know what? I'm totes okay with that. If knowing what I want makes me a bitch, then so be it. Knowing what you want sounds easy, right? But sometimes you need to do a little work to figure it out, and *own it*. It took me a few years to tap into my own inner boss bitch and learn to find my voice. You know—that thing that makes you *you*. Your style, your brand, your *je ne sais quoi*, as the French say. Because those bitches always say it best.

So, based on my history as Bossy Stassi and my deep-seated *annoying* love of attention, as you might guess, my boss bitch tendencies showed up at a very early age.

Like many of you, I had (and still have, BTW) a passion for the Spice Girls. I get excited every time one of their songs comes on, and any reunion-tour gossip turns me into a delirious thirteen-year-old fangirl. Like, seriously, I need to be sedated. If you need proof of my obsession, at age nine I would diligently memorize dance routines to Spice Girls songs and hold my own auditions during recess for my own New Orleans Spice Girls crew. Some kids didn't make the cut, which had the parents all up in arms if their precious snowflakes were left out. But that's just life, right? *Don't even get me started on the whole "every kid gets a participation trophy" thing.* I knew early on that if you want something to happen you need to *make* it happen yourself. You don't just get a trophy for showing up.

Still, I can't say I "found my voice" until a few years after my Spice Girls crew had disbanded. My big moment didn't happen until I traveled to Los Angeles one summer as a fifteen-year-old musical-theater hopeful with a Doritos chip on her shoulder.

As a teen, I was artsy AF. I could not have *been* more artsy—I went to a performing arts school and studied theater. I thought I was the shit—maybe because I was so successful as the dictator of a teen Spice Girls crew way back when. So during this artsy era, at the age of fifteen, my dad took me on a trip to Los Angeles. I knew I wanted to go to an acting conservatory, and my dad somehow knew Robert Redford's* acting coach. This acting coach agreed to let me sit in on one of his classes while I was in LA, even though I was some random teenage wannabe actress from Louisiana and the only starring roles I'd had

---

* It wasn't actually Robert Redford, but it was an equally intimidating older actor.

onstage were at school in New Orleans. And in my own head, obviously.

We flew out to Los Angeles—the early 2000s Los Angeles, before Sur and *Vanderpump* were even a thing. The day of the class, I got dressed in my army-green bomber jacket from Express that was two sizes too small. Side note: I had seen a pic of Sienna Miller wearing a green bomber jacket, so I squished myself into this knockoff because I felt insanely cool, like I belonged in LA, a place way more advanced, style-wise, than Louisiana. I also had on my "Free Winona" T-shirt, which I wore all the time back then because I, again, thought it made me look cool. You see the pattern here, right? Anyhow, my dad dropped me off, and I headed into the class with a bunch of adults and waited for my mind to be blown.

I don't remember a lot of things from my past because I take Xanax very seriously, but I *do* remember being in this class thinking, *I am a fifteen-year-old wannabe actor from Louisiana and even I can see that these actors are getting off too fucking easy!* New Orleans Center for Creative Arts (NOCCA), where I went to school, was *so* much more hard-core than this class. It was like a serious-ass theater boot camp where a teacher once stuck a wire hanger down my back and pressed it into my skin until I cried so I could channel the feeling of being sad/hurt/in pain. Was that borderline abusive? Sure. What does a hanger have to do with anything? No idea. But IDGAF. You have to suffer for your art, which is what I do on *Vanderpump Rules* every single day. Sort of.

Since my school was so tough, watching this California acting coach praise his students for lazy work instead of torture them with hangers made me think: *I could kill this shit.* I held my tongue and didn't blurt that out to the class, even though inside I was dying to say what I felt. Sadly, I repressed Bossy Stassi and kept quiet.

After class, the acting coach asked if I wanted to have lunch with him and Not Robert Redford. This was way before YOLO, but YOLO, so of course I said yes. Any male acting coach taking a young, impressionable teenage girl to lunch probably expects her to look pretty, smile, and tell him how amazing he is even if his class was lame AF and he was having them do that ridiculous "falling game" where people fall into your arms so you can learn to trust your partner. Gross. But when the time came for this guy to ask me what I thought, as Not Robert looked on, instead of kissing his ass, something came over me and I blurted, "I thought it kind of sucked." And then I proceeded to word vomit all the reasons it sucked and why my school, NOCCA, was so much better. "If you could see what we're doing in New Orleans with wire hangers you would understand. . . ."

Awkward teenage boss move! Maybe my burst of confidence came from my too-tight green bomber jacket or my "Free Winona" shirt. Who knows. The way Not Robert and the coach stared at me as I spewed out all the reasons they sucked definitely made me physically uncomfortable, but I just kept on talking. Let's just say the rest of the lunch was not the most ideal, but I survived, and so did they. Unless they've had to undergo years of therapy because of my speech. Egos in LA are very fragile, so it's totally plausible.

We managed to finish the lunch, and when my dad picked me up and asked how it went, I told him what happened. That I, Bossy Stassi, told this famous actor that his coach's class sucked and that he could learn a thing or two if he came to my performing arts high school in New Orleans. My dad was quiet, so I assumed he was embarrassed that his teenage daughter had sabotaged her future and insulted two grown men in the process.

Later on that night, my dad surprised me and told me how proud he was of what I had done. He said, "I need you to always say what you're thinking because there's so much power in that." That's always stuck with me (which is why saying shit without a filter is pretty much standard for me). As my dad said all this, I remember thinking, "Eff yeah. A fifteen-year-old girl's opinion matters." I mean, I *didn't* learn much in the fancy LA class and I was just stating a personal truth that might have made some grown men uncomfortable—but hey, sometimes the truth hurts!

So whatever age you are (or pretend you are), your opinion does matter, regardless of how different or "weird" it is. You want to write a song about caramel lattes and how great they are? Do it. You want to tell some Nobel Prize winners how much you love brunch with bottomless mimosas? Go ahead. You want to spew a bunch of stuff about how much you love the Spice Girls while you're on a first date with a classical guitar player who's won a few Grammys (I have done this on plenty of dates, FYI)?

Be my guest—because if they don't think your opinion matters, no matter how basic it is, they're not worth it. And being Next Level Basic is all about being true to yourself and having confidence, no matter what a bunch of haters say. So find your voice, whether you're fifteen or thirty-five or fifty-two. Call people out if they deserve it, stand up for your basic beliefs, and never, ever let them crush your basic bitch *boss* spirit.

Next Level Basic TAKEAWAY

Being basic means being true to what *you* like, without caving to the pressure of being "cool" or "edgy" or whatever basic-haters are into. So before you can truly embrace the basic lifestyle (with pride), you have to find your voice. I first had to learn to speak up and speak out before I could go full basic, and that meant not being scared to tell two grown professional men that I thought their class was lame. That one breakthrough moment gave me the confidence I needed to keep speaking out, whether it's about my love of musical theater or my passion for outfit-of-the-day (OOTD) selfies. The next time you find yourself holding back and self-censoring because you're afraid of what someone might think—open your mouth and get your opinion out there! And I promise, the confidence you get will help you take your basicness to the next level.

THE "LET'S GET REAL" CHALLENGE

To get you on the path to finding your own basic 2.0 voice, I challenge you to share a photo and a mini essay (like really mini, 140 characters or less) on Instagram or Twitter that's about something basic AF that you *love*—but that you've been afraid to admit. Share it, tag me, and use #NextLevelBasicChallenge, and we'll see how many likes and YAS QUEENS you rack up. Having basic tastes is nothing to be ashamed of; it's something that should be celebrated! And I support you.

In fact, here's an uncensored list of my own basic obsessions as inspiration.

▶ **PHOTO BOOTHS:** A party with a photo booth is a true party for me. Literally everyone looks better in a photo-booth photo as opposed to an iPhone pic or a photo from a regular camera (which no one does anymore unless they're a professional photographer or they're seventy-five years old). The lighting in photo booths is amazing; you're usually drunk, so you look relaxed, glowy, and/or ridiculous; and I love the cute borders and props—it's so freakin' festive. Sign me up.

▶ **SPRAY TANS:** I don't want to damage my skin, but I still want to fake-bake so that I can totes look exotic, even in

December. You just have to find a place that doesn't turn you orange like the photos in *Us Weekly*'s "Too Tan Stars" photo gallery or *People*'s "Orange You Tan!" list, and you're good.

▶ **BILLBOARD TOP 20 MUSIC:** There's a reason these songs are in the Top 20 . . . It's because they're catchy AF, and millions of people think so. It's a bonding experience to be at a party or a bar with a bunch of strangers and hear everyone sing along to the same Bieber song. I own my musical taste, and I'll blare Top 20 as loudly as I want to, thanks very much.

▶ *SEX AND THE CITY:* Yeah, the show is old now, but I watch every single episode *and* both movies when they come on TV as if I've never seen them before. Personally, I think I'm all four characters combined: I tend to be cynical, and I try to hide my softer side—like Miranda. I can be a bit power-obsessed, and I love a good vibrator/romp sesh—like Samantha (listen, a girl has got to get hers). A feminine/classic outfit always does it for me, *and* I often have a stick up my ass—like Charlotte. And, finally, being surrounded by fashion/shoes/clothes makes me feel like I've popped a Xanax and I am the center of the freaking universe—like Carrie. . . . *But*, for realzies though, Miranda is my spirit animal. That chick worked 24-7, ate a brownie out of the garbage can, and always unapologetically told the truth. Mad respect, Miranda. This show will never get old, IMHO. In fact, I recently went on a girls' trip to wine country, and we all had to do "dares." One of the dares was for Ariana Madix to go up to a man in a cowboy hat and ask to take a photo with the hat on. Turns out, it was freaking *Aidan* from *Sex and the City*. I've never been more disappointed that I wasn't the one who got that dare. I was the girl who got dared to do burpees. FML. Missed. Effing. Opportunity.

▶ **EAT PRAY LOVE:** I watch this movie every time I'm about to go on a trip abroad. It just really gets me into that free-spirited, adventurous headspace. So what if it's cheesy and over-the-top and ridiculous? Deal with it.

▶ **MONOGRAMMED EVERYTHING:** No, seriously. I have mono-grams on E.V.E.R.Y.T.H.I.N.G. I love anything personalized. Maybe it's because I grew up in the South, where your clothes and towels and bags and hats are monogrammed since (before) birth. Maybe it's just because I like the look of my initials. My love of monograms didn't do me any favors when I walked around Europe with a giant "SS" on the back of my trench coat though. That was a mistake. But more on that later.

▶ **FALL-THEMED EVERYTHING:** When the first day of autumn rolls around, I don't care how hot it is outside, I bust out the over-the-knee boots, sweater dresses, Halloween decorations, fall-scented candles, and I google the nearest pumpkin patch. I can't get enough of everything fall-related. I want apple cider. I want to spend the whole month of October watching *Hocus Pocus* on repeat. Haunted hayride? Yes, please.

▶ **PINTEREST:** I just can't quit it. Home decor, fashion ideas, hairstyles, makeup inspo, bridal shit (no, I'm not engaged), travel locations, funny memes, recipes (not that I cook). I fall into a dark Pinterest hole way more often than I would like to admit. Before we were on *Vanderpump Rules*, Katie Maloney and I were broke AF. So to entertain ourselves we would sit around the apartment and Pinterest together, whether it was making boards for our future weddings or boards for fashion. Little did we know, several years later, we'd be on a reality show together.

▶ **BEDAZZLED SHOES:** I. HAVE. A. PROBLEM. I see a jewel/gem/rhinestone on a shoe and it makes me feel like I just struck oil. I totally get that they walk a fine line between being chic or tacky, but I just can't help myself. My friends and boyfriend make fun of me 24-7, but sparkly things are like an antidepressant. Basically, it's like Prozac on my feet, but cuter.

▶ **MEGHAN MARKLE:** Hi, my name is Stassi Schroeder, and I'm a Markle addict. Every basic bitch loves Meghan Markle. Why? Because she's perfect. Like, holy-crap-how-does-she-even-exist perfect. Whenever I meet someone who doesn't like her, I know they're just being a hipstery contrarian. What's not to love? She's stunning; she seems so kind; she has impeccable taste; her voice is that of an angel's. At age eleven, she wrote a letter about a sexist Ivory dishwashing liquid commercial, and her letter got megacorporation Procter & Gamble to change their thinking! She also wrote letters about it to then first lady Hillary Clinton and feminist lawyer Gloria Allred, just to cover her bases. Do you know what I was doing at eleven? Begging my parents to buy me clothes from Limited Too so that I could be "cool." Meghan Markle has achieved *royalty* against all the odds. When I can't sleep at night, I literally google Meghan Markle until

I pass out. She should maybe consider filing a restraining order.

So be a boss bitch and *own* everything you do, even if you're listening to Bieber while sitting in a monogrammed robe, watching *Sex and the City*, googling Meghan Markle until you pass out. Embracing your basic impulses is the first step to getting Next Level Basic. So get to it.

CHAPTER 2

Why Musical Theater Is Cool AF

inky Boots changed my life. So did *Aida, Les Misérables, Phantom of the Opera, Chicago*—and don't even get me started on *Moulin Rouge!* (or do, because I love that freaking movie and I can convince anyone to love it too because I'm like a Jehovah's Witness of musicals). I know there are a lot of people out there who *hate* (or think they hate) musical theater because they believe it's boring or annoying or lame to hear a bunch of people spontaneously break into song. But musical theater is cool AF, whether it's the big-budget Hollywood movie version or the stage version. And I can prove it.

As a kid, my dad introduced me to musical theater and took me to see *Les Misérables*, and it was love at first tear-your-heartstrings/make-you-want-to-burst-into-tears song. Then in eighth grade I saw *Moulin Rouge!*, starring Nicole Kidman and Ewan McGregor, for the first time, and I immediately fell into a depression because my life wasn't as romantic and amazing as the movie. They twirl on rooftops singing Elton John while declaring their everlasting love. My life in New Orleans was nothing like that, so I became obsessed. After the movie *Avatar* came out I remember reading stories about people having the "*Avatar* blues," where they got seriously depressed because life wasn't like the movie—a gorgeous alien world with giant blue people and no traffic or pollution or jury duty. Well, I got the "*Moulin Rouge!* blues," for realzies.

That movie has influenced me when it comes to every single person I've ever dated in my life. Ewan was a brooding writer, and I always fall for artistic, emotional Pisces guys. Even Jax Taylor, believe it or not, is an emotional Cancer (and also an emotional terrorist). When he showed me his old sketches and drawings, I felt like Nicole Kidman must have felt when she saw Ewan's character singing on a rooftop or typing frantically on his old-school typewriter. I loved his artistic side—but obviously Jax didn't live up to the *Moulin Rouge!* hype.

The most recent musical that I've loved on-screen was the movie *La La Land*. (Onstage my most recent obsession is— like many humans—*Hamilton*.) I *almost* got the *Moulin Rouge!* blues after I saw *La La Land* for the first time, and I *did* become obsessed, but I'm older and wiser and I've learned how to control myself just a little bit more these days. The first time I saw it in the theater (I saw it a total of six times, if you want to know how seriously I take this shit) I cried during the very first scene. Then I forced my entire family in New Orleans to cut Christmas dinner short because I'd rented out a small theater just so I could sit next to my grandmother and watch her face as she watched the movie, which was for real one of the highlights of my life. If that's not taking your basicness to the next level, I don't know what is.

Everyone has their own version of musical theater—something you're totally passionate about but something that most people say is lame. But deeply loving something that other people think is lame or cheesy is nothing to be ashamed of, even if you're blaring "Don't Cry for Me Argentina" from *Evita* as you drive to buy some basic AF cheeseburgers from In-N-Out. Every once in a while, a musical like *Hamilton* comes along that's so popular and amazing that even hard-core theater haters have to admit they love it. But, for some reason, even though there's artistry behind musical theater, it's never been considered "cool." I mean, there's a reason we're referred to as "theater nerds" in high school (and into adulthood). Musicals exist to make us feel happy, to make us cry, or to make us want to sing at the top of our lungs. At the most basic level, they make us *feel*. And that, my friends, is nothing to be ashamed of!

On that note, the only musical that I *do* think sucks is *Rent*, because the movie version came out and everyone suddenly thought they were musical-theater scholars because they knew one song that Rosario Dawson sang. (This is me being a basic-ass contrarian because I actually like *Rent*, I just don't like that the movie version overshadowed the stage version.) So, actually, *Mamma Mia!* is the one musical I can't take. It's the worst kind of basic bitch musical, but if you love it, then cheers to you. Take it to the next level by embracing that shit and never looking back.

I for real don't understand the argument that "musical theater isn't real life" so therefore it's dumb or unwatchable. How do people watch a movie about aliens or dinosaurs or giant blue people? That shit isn't real life either. Is *Game of Thrones* real life? Unfortunately for *me*, no. Yes, it's violent AF and it was a horrible time for women's rights, but that doesn't stop me from wanting to be Khaleesi IRL. I mean, millions of people watch *Game of Thrones*, so how is two people breaking into song in a musical any less real than a White Walker? Plus, musicals make you *feel* so much more than just watching two people talking on a couch—so how is that a bad thing? You can listen to the songs as therapy for any type of situation too: If you just got a new job and you're so happy you feel like doing butt-ass-naked cartwheels down the street, there's a song for you. Or if you're depressed AF because you got ghosted after what you thought was a *Moulin Rouge!*–level date, there's a song for that too.

My ex-boyfriend Patrick broke up with me on our fourth anniversary, and all I wanted to do was listen to "On My Own" from *Les Mis* on repeat and sob—*and it was the best breakup remedy ever*. Remember in the *Sex and the City* movie when Carrie goes on her honeymoon trip to Mexico with her friends after Big ditches her at the altar? I had prepaid for a four-day anniversary trip for us to Mexico, and when Patrick dumped me my friends Danni Baird from *Southern Charm* (whose engagement had just been called off) and Rachael O'Brien came with me instead. All I did was sit in the hotel room closet listening to "On My Own" and crying. (I'm sure my friends were totes happy they came.) Anyway, it helped, and after a few days of sobbing in the closet, I started to feel a little bit better. So to prove that there is a musical-theater song for every situation and emotion on the planet *and* that these songs can change your life (or help you get over a breakup), I put together a playlist just for you (*you're welcome*).

Next Level Basic MUSICAL THEATER PLAYLIST

▶ "One Day More," *Les Misérables*: This is one of my *absolute* favorites, and I am not ashamed to admit that the movie version is my favorite, as I am probably the only person in the world who loved watching (and hearing) Russell Crowe sing.

▶ "Another Day of Sun," *La La Land*: Legit any emotion I've ever felt, this song fits. I don't care if I'm happy, sad, angry . . . it works for everything.

▶ "The Phantom of the Opera": So suspenseful and powerful. I get all weird and pretend I'm in a dungeony cave when I listen to this.

▶ "On My Own," *Les Misérables*: Sad AF, but who doesn't love a good cry? Great breakup song if you're a masochist.

▶ "My Strongest Suit," *Aida*: It's like this song was carefully orchestrated for the fashionista drama queens of the world. Literally a song about how her outfits are the best thing about her. #Goals.

▶ "Written in the Stars," *Aida*: Such a good love song. *So* intense. That Elton John knows what's up.

▶ "I Know the Truth," *Aida*: As you can see I am a huge *Aida* nerd, so it was incredibly hard to narrow the songs down. This is *the* best song to sing at the top of your lungs around the house, in the car, in a meadow . . .

▶ "All That Jazz," *Chicago*: Classic. Classic. Classic. Plus it was the first song I ever performed in "The World Goes 'Round" showcase when I was fifteen, so it's near and dear to my heart.

▶ "Cell Block Tango," *Chicago*: A bunch of baller-ass women singing about how they murdered their husbands? Sign me up.

▶ "Defying Gravity," *Wicked*: Ugh, so uplifting and amazing. Seriously makes me want to find a way to scientifically defy gravity.

▶ "Maybe This Time," *Cabaret*: This is a good one for when you've been single a wee bit long. Like the moment you realize you haven't had sex in six months.

▶ "You Must Love Me," *Evita*: For everyone out there who just really needs attention and positive affirmation (which is all of us, right?).

▶ "Don't Cry for Me Argentina," *Evita*: Another classic. Also makes me feel all powerful and shit, like one day I could maybe run for president?

▶ "Let Me Entertain You," *Gypsy*: Not to brag, but I won Most Talented in my senior high school class partly for playing Gypsy Rose Lee. Are you gagging yet?

▶ "I Hate Men," *Kiss Me, Kate*: I love a song that's meant for a drunk cynic.

▶ "At the Ballet," *A Chorus Line*: Super beautiful, super heart-wrenching, super awesome.

▶ "There Are Worse Things I Could Do," *Grease*: I always loved Rizzo. She is tough, she is vulnerable, she probably went from being a Pink Lady to being a boss bitch somewhere.

▶ "Come What May," *Moulin Rouge!*: All right, just thinking about this song is bringing on the waterworks. I mean, lovers who can't be together so they have a secret song? Supes romantic.

▶ "Nature Boy," *Moulin Rouge!*: The opening song in *Moulin Rouge!* I can't quite put my finger on why it's one of my favorites, maybe because I've watched the movie 2,348,234 times and I know what's to come, or maybe it's just that beautiful of a song.

▶ "Bye Bye Baby," *Gentlemen Prefer Blondes*: This one seems a little random, but give it a chance. It makes me want to go on a fancy-ass cruise.

▶ "Over the Rainbow," *The Wizard of Oz*: I can't make a list of songs without including this one. It's universally adored. I dare you to try to find one person who doesn't like it. And if they say they don't they're definitely lying.

▶ "Ding-Dong! The Witch Is Dead," *The Wizard of Oz*: I always felt bad that so many people were cheerily singing about the witch dying. Like WTF?

▶ "You'll Be Back," *Hamilton*: If I were in Hamilton I would totally play King George and sing this song. "*I will kill your friends and family to remind you of my love . . .*" I mean, come on.

Musical theater might be basic but it's also kind of weird, so full-on embracing it instead of hiding it and only listening when you're alone and the door is locked is Next Level Basic. Your weirdness makes you you, so why not take it up a notch? If you're into smooth jazz, do it all the way and tell everyone about your love of Yanni. Millions of people love Marvel movies and I personally don't care for them, but if you love Captain America, then embrace that shit by wearing a Captain America T-shirt out on a Saturday night. And I challenge you to listen to this playlist and *not* love it. Listen at full volume with the windows down for maximum effect.

Next Level Basic TAKEAWAY

Imagine if I had suppressed my love of musical theater with all of its dramatic ups and downs and emotional peaks and valleys— would I have stayed in New Orleans and become a math teacher (not that there's anything wrong with that, besides the fact that I hate math)? Would I have never become a *Vanderpump* star? You never know where your basic tendencies will take you, so hiding them won't do anyone any good—especially not you. Maybe you *love* algebra or physics but feel like it's a lame thing to gush about at parties. But what if gushing about algebra leads you to your dream career or allows you to meet someone who loves math as much as you do and you make a lifelong BFF? Musical theater inspired me to *study* theater, which then led me to live in Los Angeles, which then led me to reality TV. If I hadn't been basic AF from day one with this stuff, I might be singing *Aida* songs secretly in the shower, always wondering what could have been. . . .

CHAPTER 3

The Cult of Stassi

irst off, actual cults are scary AF. Charles Manson, Jim Jones, David Koresh—they're all truly psychotic and they did terrible, unforgivable things, so before you start hate-tweeting me and calling me an evil witch, just know that I'm not condoning them at all. Seriously, what kind of monster do you think I am?

That said, I dream of one day starting my own cult. But I wouldn't be like these evil, narcissistic maniacs. I mean, Jim Jones made his followers drink Kool-Aid mixed with cyanide and Valium. Personally, I don't know why he chose gross Kool-Aid instead of a laced Moscow Mule or Kir Royale, which would have been much more humane because at least they would have gone out with a buzz. And Charles Manson was a weirdo man-child who moved to Los Angeles to become a famous musician, but when that didn't happen he decided to get attention by forming a murderous cult instead—*and it worked.* If *I* formed a cult I would keep it light (no murder or Kool-Aid) and just manipulate people into becoming basic AF so they could live their best life. I would be more like an Oprah-type cult leader—benevolent, anti murder, and very pro bread.

My closest run-in with an actual cult was Jax Taylor's fault. It was about ten years ago when we were dating and he was living with me and pursuing a modeling career, which is so totes embarrassing. It's the most stereotypical thing I've ever heard: A twenty-two-year-old girl moves to Los Angeles and dates a model. Gross. Anyway, he came home one day and was like, "Stassi, I just did a commercial for Scientology!"

I was like, "*Pardon?*"

I understand that any job that pays is a positive, and I'm not judging that part. You've gotta pay the bills. But then he went on to say, "I talked to them about you and they want us to come in and consider Scientology." And that's when I basically fell onto the floor laughing. I was like, "Dude, are we talking about the science fiction, L. Ron Hubbard, alien movie, Tom-Cruise-couch-jumping religion?" He said yes. Jax was never the sharpest tool in the shed. I told him he was out of his freaking mind, but he kept going and said that everyone there was so supportive and they loved the fact that I was in college and they wanted to help with my career and that he thought we should give it a shot. So the wheels in my head started turning and I thought, "Actually . . . this could be fun." I decided I was going to challenge them and mess with *their* minds, so I wrote a list of questions to ask them to prove that this was all BS.

When we went to the Scientology center we met with "Tom Cruise's mentor." The guy threw out Tom Cruise's name like four hundred million times to make sure we knew who we were dealing with. As soon as we sat down in this guy's fancy-ass office I started asking questions like, *What is this place all about? What is the deal with the aliens?* Mind you, for my questions I was mainly going off "research" I got from pop-culture websites, but my main goal was to challenge this guy, so I figured asking about aliens was a legit way to go.

This bro knew how to dodge a question though. Like when I kept saying *What about the aliens?* he'd laugh and change the subject to Jax and me and the ways he could save us and make us famous and rich, like Tom I guess. After our weird-ass office visit, he walked us around the building and everyone we saw was in the happiest mood. It was . . . *like a cult*. Even the woman cleaning the floors was looking at me and smiling with the creepiest look on her face. It was like no one there had had a period or experienced a delayed flight or been through a breakup in their life. It was scary AF. Who smiles like you're on a beach in Bali with a bod like Adriana Lima when you're actually in a weird-ass building with a dirty mop in your hand?

Then Tom Cruise's mentor said Jax and I were going to be separated, and he took me into a room alone to watch a video that involved a kid eating a boiled egg and then witnessing a car accident. Years later, every time the kid smelled a boiled egg he had PTSD. As I watched, it all started to make sense to me—like this was some scientific shit. I started believing a little bit. The video was about how you could control yourself with your mind, and I definitely wanted to control myself with my mind—who doesn't? Once I was reunited with Jax I was like *Let's give this a shot.* Tom Cruise's mentor convinced us to pay $100 (each!) for a textbook, and then took us to "class," which was a room full of people of all ages, all sitting silently with their $100 textbooks. There were also kids' building blocks on the tables, and they told us we couldn't have any possessions with us at all, like no water or phone or ChapStick. They also forbade us from eating or drinking anything for several hours before any future classes, so I realized that I couldn't have a vodka soda the night before a class, which was a problem.

Everyone in class was so into it, like they full-blown drank the Kool-Aid. The creepy teacher made Jax open the textbook and read, and he couldn't pronounce one of the words (it was probably like "lamp" or "world" or "science," something really easy that freaked his brain out because it was a lot of pressure). The teacher asked him to do something with the blocks to channel his brain or commune with the aliens or something, and at that moment it got super weird and we knew we had to get out. This is when I was working at Sur, so we told her that I had to go to work immediately. Before we could escape they made us sign up for two classes, and I said, "I'm a server and I can't commit to this because I'm poor and sometimes I have to pick up shifts." So we fake signed up for some classes just to get out of there, and we left legit terrified. It was the most culty thing I have experienced in my entire life. I still have the textbook (I am not parting with that thing) and it is hella weird. None of it makes sense. I also still have my membership card, and I will never get rid of that either because it's like a collector's item.

The fact that cults are real is insane to me. It blows my mind. But the cult I want to start is not creepy—it's *fun*. I've fantasized about starting my own mind-control experiment to help people get in touch with their most basic self. Like the Cult of Oprah, this would be all about positivity and scented candles instead of death and destruction and aliens (although I do love aliens). My followers could leave the cult at any time with no consequences—*but they would totally regret it for the rest of their lives*. They could decide not to obey one of my orders—*but they would be missing out on a life-changing experience*. Because who doesn't want to spend every single day celebrating the weird and basic things that make life worth living?

And so, after years of careful research (usually at 3:00 a.m. after I've had a few bottles of wine and some animal-shaped Kraft mac 'n' cheese), I present my methods for luring people into my very own Next Level Basic cult.

▶ Mass-text followers at 3:00 a.m. and force them to take a warm shot of cheap tequila. (Being the benevolent cult leader I aim to be, I'll make sure their bars are stocked at all times.) To prove their loyalty, they have to post an Instagram story that shows them doing the shot.

▶ Demand followers go to brunch, order the healthiest thing on the menu—like a side of kale or a single apple—take a photo of it, post it on Instagram, and write #Foodie #CheatDay.

▶ Make them listen to Will Smith's "Wild Wild West" on repeat for 3.5 hours. I happen to love this song and I've been dancing to it since I was a kid. It's just a happy damn song, okay? It also happens to be my go-to hangover song, in that I listen to it when I feel like crap and need to get out of a funk. All cult leaders are trying to turn their followers into mini versions of themselves, so listening to this song accomplishes that goal.

▶ I will send them secret packages of deep-fried goat-cheese balls once a day (which is incredibly selfless of me, BTW).

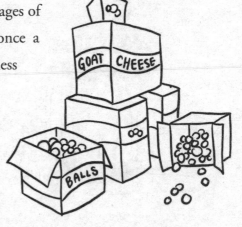

▶ I will have them take weekly tests to ensure they are watching the required television shows. Those currently being: *Game of Thrones, Real Housewives of New York City, Black Mirror, Bachelor in Paradise, 90 Day Fiancé,* and—of course—*Vanderpump Rules.* The tests will check their knowledge of the plots, the characters, the most dramatic moments (who slept with who, who slapped who, who cried and why), and the outfits that people wore. Even for *Game of Thrones. Especially* for *Game of Thrones.*

▶ I will command that followers post a heavily edited, Facetuned, filtered selfie once a month with the caption: #Blessed #NoFilter

▶ With each person's initiation and undying devotion to my cult, I will sign them up for a monthly wine subscription, paid for by me. So, *you're welcome.* I don't even think Oprah is *that* generous. She just picks out expensive candles and tells you to buy them with your own money. I would

never be that cruel. Creating a cult would help me live out my Bossy Stassi childhood fantasies, and I would also be doing humanity a great service by helping people get on the path to discovering their most basic selves.

Next Level Basic TAKEAWAY

So the point of my cult isn't fame or power or murder or anything—it's to help people live a Next Level Basic lifestyle without shame. Since day one of *Vanderpump Rules*, Lisa has always told us that her goal was for each of us to find what we were good at and flourish. She has always pushed us to be successful, and some very sound advice I received from her was to embrace what I loved or what I knew or what I was good at. I quickly realized that embracing who I was helped me connect to people, and it then brought me a podcast and now this book. Lisa definitely inspired me to be myself. You're never going to see me writing a cookbook or coming out with a pop song. Those just aren't my strengths. But acting like a benevolent cult leader and helping people channel their own basic self? That's me.

CHAPTER 4

Obsessed

Everybody has their *thing*. That one thing that you're into that's maybe a little weird or quirky or so basic that it becomes next level, like loving Harry Potter so much you read each book and watched each movie twenty-six times (as an adult), or being so into *Titanic* that you got a tattoo of the Heart of the Ocean blue-diamond necklace on your ass. Def not sure if anyone has done that, but if you have—congrats! You are truly living your best Next Level Basic life.

As for me, anyone who follows me on Twitter or Instagram knows I'm pretty into lighthearted things like murder, the supernatural, and death. It's kind of my thing. I like to randomly AirDrop scary clown pics to strangers, I make sure

I'm always following exactly 666 people on social media, and I make my own DIY Ouija boards out of bottle caps and pieces of cardboard (*and they work*). I fantasize about having a pet zombie (I've watched a lot of *The Walking Dead*) and my iPhone's name is Satan. I'm not a freaking Satan worshipper, but I am a little obsessed—and I'm okay with it. The sad thing about basic obsessions is that so many of us hide them because we're afraid of what the haters might say. But I've come to embrace my love of all things sinister and evil because, well . . . it makes me freaking happy.

Maybe my love of the dark side comes from the fact that I grew up in New Orleans, which is a city that's famous for spirits and voodoo and aboveground graves. Some of my childhood birthday parties were haunted tours of the city instead of bounce houses or Chuck E. Cheese's, and my college thesis was on New Orleans "voodoo queen" Marie Laveau. I don't think you can live in New Orleans and not have at least a small interest in darkness. I recently asked my dad where my love for all of this weird shit comes from and he said, "The Haunted Mansion ride at Disneyland." It's still my favorite ride. But it didn't stop with the Haunted Mansion. My parents divorced when I was five, and my brother and I alternated nights with our parents, and when we were at Dad's house we always wanted to watch *Army of Darkness*, which is probably one of the top five weirdest movies for children to watch. (Side note: *Beetlejuice* was also another one of my childhood fave movies, and while other kids were watching

Rugrats, I was watching *Tales from the Crypt,* so pretty sure I was just doomed from the start.)

Then as I got older I became obsessed with all of M. Night Shyamalan's movies. *Signs* was major for me because it combined three of my obsessions: M. Night Shyamalan, aliens, and Joaquin Phoenix. I love those brooding emotional types, so I was obsessed with Joaquin in *Signs* like I was obsessed with Ewan McGregor in *Moulin Rouge!* When I was a teen, my dad continued to enable my obsessions. One morning he woke me up extra early for school (I was obviously pissed). He told me to get in the car and then drove me to Blockbuster (remember those? RIP), and on the wall outside was the biggest *Signs* poster I'd ever seen besides, like, a billboard on the side of the road. (Mind you, billboards in New Orleans were never for movies . . . think more gumbo or Saints vibes, but you get the picture—this thing was *big*.) At six in the morning I sat there and watched my dad gently rip this poster off the wall so I could put it on *my* bedroom wall. I'm sure what he was doing was illegal, but I was not complaining. Also, shout-out to my dad for being so badass that he would embrace my weirdness enough to commit a mild crime. TRULY NEXT LEVEL, folks.

That *Signs* poster is long gone, but my childhood obsession with darkness has not disappeared, and if anything, it's just gotten weirder and more Next Level Basic. On *Vanderpump* season five I had to make a dating profile, and I was like, *Fuck it, I'm not going to sugarcoat anything; I'm just going to be who I am!* I didn't do a bio and instead I just answered the "likes" questions as honestly as I could. My list was not really what you'd think guys in LA would be super into since it was:

Stassi's Likes

Ghosts	Shopping
Musicals	Ranch dressing
Murder	Did I say ghosts?
Cemeteries	Aliens
The color sky blue	Hot sauce
Gold	Online shopping
Anything sparkly	Dogs
Shoes	*Game of Thrones*
Serial killers	Kate Hudson movies
Day drinking	Shoes again
Brunch	Haunted houses

I don't know anyone who has gotten that many likes and messages. Every single person who wrote back was like "This is the most authentic dating profile I've ever seen—*marry me*." I eventually deleted the account because I only signed up because I had to for *Vanderpump*, and the responses were pretty overwhelming. I mean, I wanted to meet people with equally twisted interests, but online you never know if someone likes murder in a cheeky way, or if they are actually a serial killer. After the online-dating experience, I realized that everyone *is* just a weird-ass obsessive like me, but usually they're just hiding their weirdness. That's sad to me. I *want* to know your quirks and basic AF tendencies because they're interesting, so why pretend?

This is the thing. I have a million books on witchcraft. I grew up with my mom and my aunt always doing the Ouija board and it never scared me. When I was about eight or nine years old they let me do it with them, and my brother and I would always have my aunt in the room with us just in case shit got crazy. You need to be respectful while you're doing the Ouija board (real talk— I never know how to pronounce it—*Ouijay, Ouijee, Ouijuh* . . . please tweet at me if you know how to say this word). FYI, pretty much all the spirits that go through Ouija boards are spirits that are fucking with you. You can't channel someone you know like your sweet granny because the spirits going through the board are like cynical pranksters. Some are evil, and some are like, *I'm bored, so I'm going to mess with this asshole's mind.* That's the way I look at it. Maybe I sound like a freakin' lunatic right now, but it's true.

I do believe there's a connection with the spirit world, and I have proven that this isn't a bullshit thing with my friends. When they would doubt me, if I didn't have a Ouija board handy, I would make my own with a piece of cardboard, a marker, and a bottle cap as the planchette (that thing that moves around on the board). Then I would tell them, "Ask a question in your head and don't say it out loud." Then they would go one by one and ask a random-ass question like *What my dad's middle name?* or *What's my boyfriend's favorite flower?* And sure enough, my DIY board would start spelling out the right answer and everyone would freak out. Once we were done I would rip that board into a million pieces and be done with it. You do not mess around with the Ouija.

Besides the Ouija board, there was one time when my obsession got *real*.

I was out drinking with my friend Katie Maloney from *Vanderpump* and her friend Jennifer, and we were bonding, not over guys but over ghosts. She said, "Have you ever heard of the Los Feliz murder house?" I was immediately intrigued. So we left a party at midnight and drove to the Los Feliz neighborhood of Los Angeles, which has these amazing old Hollywood homes that only people like Angelina Jolie and Ryan Gosling can afford. So we stop the car, and there is the most grand, scary-ass Spanish-style home in the world sitting atop a hill overlooking the city: terrifying AF. The story was that there was a family living there in 1959 and one night the husband murdered the wife in her sleep with a hammer and then went into his eldest daughter Judye's room. Judye woke up and ran to get her siblings (like a badass), and they escaped to a neighbor's house. The dad killed himself, and the kids ran away and were supposedly raised by an aunt somewhere. There's also a rumor that another family rented the house after the murders and then fled the house on the anniversary of the attack and just disappeared. WTF!

So of course, I wanted to look in all the windows, and inside the house I saw a ton of old furniture that made it look like no one had lived there since 1959, which was super creepy. I became obsessed with the house and decided that one day I was going to buy it and live there. My idea of the perfect house is an old Spanish-style vintage white house. Even if I can't have central AC, that's my dream. But a haunted house on top of that? Sign me up. It doesn't scare me, because I've developed my own coping mechanism so I can enjoy this dark stuff and not get scared: I just imagine there's a powerful force field around me that shields me from any real harm. It might not be rational, but it works.

So after I talked about the murder house on my podcast I got tweets from listeners saying that the house was for sale for $2.8 million (it was cheap as far as mansions go because people were murdered there, obvi). I was not in a position to buy that house at all, so this was basically my worst nightmare. I wondered if I should start a GoFundMe account to pay for it (I *seriously* considered this option). Then I asked my dad and grandma if they wanted to invest. I thought of every possible way to get that house, short of stripping, but I realized it wasn't in the cards. Then one morning Jennifer called me at seven, and why I answered is still a mystery. I hate talking on the phone, and I basically just use my phone to stalk people on Instagram. But I picked up, and she said that she contacted the real estate agent and made an appointment to view the house that afternoon.

I made up every excuse: *I have to get my nails done! I have to get a spray tan! I'm hungry! I have to feed my dogs! I have to contour my face . . .* Then half an hour later, when I ran out of excuses, I was like, *Stassi—this is your year of* yes. *You have the chance to see this house, so don't be a wuss.* So I told Jennifer that I needed her to google "Buying Houses for Dummies" and write down bullet points for me so I could memorize them and method-act the shit out of this appointment. I'm a terrible liar, plus I felt guilty that a real estate person had to waste their time with me when they could be at happy hour or actually selling a house. It made me feel like an asshole, but I also had an overwhelming need to see this house, so I decided being an asshole for an hour was worth it.

I put on the most businesslike outfit and the most expensive shoes and purse I owned so it looked like I could afford the house. Jennifer and I took a tequila shot before going in, and one of the first things the agent said was "Are you aware of the history of the house?" I told her it didn't bother me at all. We walked up the grand staircase, and when she got to the door the keys wouldn't work. She said, "This hasn't ever happened to me before," and so I immediately wondered if something was telling me not to go in there. Finally she got the door open and I walked in and saw that all the old furniture had been cleaned out, and the whole first floor was painted the same color I always choose for my apartments. It's the lightest shade of blue. I call it "Stassi blue," which sounds crazy narcissistic, but whatever.

The tour kept getting weirder, because when I walked into the eldest daughter Judye's room I saw a light switch plate that read "Judye" with little flowers on it, and it looked like there were bloodstains on it—I kid you not. FOR REAL. Then the basement of the house was like a scene out of the movie *Saw*—dark and creepy with weird-looking tools and rusty pipes all over the place, like a room you would torture someone in. It was terrifying, but I wanted the house so badly I convinced myself and the agent that I was going to buy it. (Now that I'm thinking about it, I kinda feel like I deserve an award of some kind.) Then, as we're walking back down the grand staircase, we pass the superheavy wooden front door (like so heavy you would need a wrecking crew to get this thing down), and as soon as I passed by the door I heard a loud *bang!* and screaming. So right after I walked past it, the door flung open and Jennifer and the agent went screaming in different directions. They were so freaked out that they wanted to leave immediately. I could have stayed all day (and night, and forever), but sadly we left. The next morning I found out it sold for $2.3 million. Ironically a podcast listener messaged me and said their mom was the one who bought the house. What are the odds of that? I still feel like one day I will own that house, and so I just hope that listener's mom isn't demolishing the haunted front door or ruining the charmingly terrifying basement.

Obviously, it's not good to be *too* obsessed with one thing (a person, a drug, a love of gore and ghosts). But healthy obsessions are just that—healthy. Everybody needs something to be passionate about, so if you don't have that thing yet, it's time to start looking for your very own Los Feliz murder house to (pretend to) buy. And if you *do* have a basic obsession that you're afraid to share with the world—screw that! Let everyone know about it, because who cares if they make fun of your *Titanic* tattoo or your hidden shrine to Harry Potter? It's *your* obsession, so embrace it. Who cares what the haters say?

Next Level Basic TAKEAWAY

Instead of repressing my love of horror and murder, I embraced the hell out of it and basically let it become like a personality calling card. It makes it easy for people to get me gifts (give me serial killer–themed shot glasses or a scary clown doll and I'm happy), and it gives me something to get excited about year-round, since there's always a horror film coming out or a crazy ghost story to tell. So if you have that weird quirk that your friends don't understand, don't hide it—make it your *thing*. If you're confident about it, it'll become one of those interesting facts that help define you, like, "That's Melissa, she's into baking, caramel lattes, and collecting serial-killer memorabilia." Trust me, no one will forget Melissa, and they'll find her fascinating AF.

STASSI'S FAVORITE* SERIAL KILLERS

One of my favorite things to do when I'm bored (besides google Meghan Markle) is to go to the Wikipedia page entitled "List of Serial Killers by Number of Victims." Then I click on a random name and learn about what they did and who they were. I also own the official *Encyclopedia of Serial Killers* (the second edition). I understand how insane I sound, but I'm just freakin' fascinated by how insane these murderers are. As much as I like reading about these psychos, I'm a sensitive wuss who gets queasy when I get my blood drawn. . . .

So, in no particular order, I present:

▶ **THEODORE ROBERT BUNDY, AKA TED BUNDY:** I mean, he looked like the JFK of serial killers. (And now Zac Efron is playing him in a movie—be still, my basic heart.) At one point he kept a bunch of severed heads in his apartment, and he escaped jail *twice*. Like, WHAT?! I also love that he was executed exactly seven months after my birth. Justice.

▶ **JACK THE RIPPER:** Okay, he's the most infamous basic-ass serial killer for a reason. He's like the equivalent of Top 40

---

* Take the word "favorite" with a grain of salt, please. I'm not trying to glorify these mass murderers!

music . . . and he only killed five (known) people! This guy murdered five prostitutes, starting in 1888 in London, got away with it, and he is now the subject of a million movies, shows, books, and articles. He put in the bare minimum of serial killing and became the most famous one of all. Now that I think of it, he's like a reality star: Put in the bare minimum amount of work and reap the rewards. If he were alive today he totally would be doing sponsored Instagram posts.

▶ **JEFFREY LIONEL DAHMER:** This guy ate his victims. I repeat, HE ATE HIS VICTIMS. (Side note: I'm eating Italian salami as I type this and it's grossing me out.) Dahmer was also discharged from the military for "heavy drinking." The man loved a good happy hour, so . . . we have that in common. He also had this idea to drill holes in his victims' heads and pour some shit in there to make real-life "zombies." Snaps for creativity, but glad he's dead.

▶ **AILEEN WUORNOS:** I think my fascination with Aileen is because I'm a basic bitch who loves Charlize Theron, who played Aileen in the movie *Monster*. But also, there aren't many female serial killers so . . . nice work?

▶ **THE AXEMAN OF NEW ORLEANS:** No one could ever figure out who this bro was! The murders started in 1910, when a man was breaking into homes and killing people with their own axes. Nine years after that, the New Orleans newspaper the *Times-Picayune* published a letter from the "Axeman," where he said he was a demon from the hottest hell and that on March 19, he was going to go out and murder some more people, but if you were playing jazz music loudly, he'd bypass your home. I mean, that is some weird-ass almost-biblical shit. March 19 rolled around, everyone played their jazz music, and no one got killed. Weird AF. Like, if I decided to go out and murder, I'd be like, "All right, people of West Hollywood, if you're not playing musical theater, Pitbull, or Will Smith tonight, you're done for!"

▶ **ELIZABETH BÁTHORY:** Picture a pretty, regal Marie Antoinette–type serial killer. Elizabeth was a Hungarian noblewoman born in 1560 who is said to have tortured and murdered more than 650 people . . . because she was bored! Like, she is for real in the Guinness World Records for being the most prolific female murderer. I'm not going to go into detail about what she did to her victims, because you might vomit up your pizza and ranch. So just google this ho in your own time, because she was *cray.*

▶ **JOHN WAYNE GACY JR.:** He is pretty much why we are all terrified of clowns. He was known as the "Killer Clown" because he would dress up as Pogo the Clown for children's events. That's next-level scary. Never trust a clown, people.

▶ **ED GEIN:** This is the dude who inspired the movies *Psycho* and *The Texas Chainsaw Massacre*, so he totes couldn't be left off this list. (I personally feel bad that he's so famous, yet no one knows his name. Like, what a waste of all that murdering.) He would go to local cemeteries, exhume graves, and use the body parts to—wait for it—decorate his home. *Architectural Digest*, where you at?

▶ **JOHN EDWARD ROBINSON:** As the first Internet serial killer who met his victims online, this guy was a trailblazer. This is the type of man we need to warn our kids about. No talking to strangers online! Side note, his screen name was "Slavemaster," so you would think that would be a giveaway. Sorry, but if anyone messaged me online with that name, it'd be a *hard no* for me. This dude is still alive . . . so I don't want to talk *too* much shit about him for fear of my own safety.

▶ **CHARLES MANSON:** While his culting skills were inspiring, I've always had this very intense hatred for Manson. So many things I can't handle: a swastika tattoo on his forehead, killing a nine-months-pregnant Sharon Tate . . . I almost didn't even want to put him on this list, but you can't have a serial-killer list without Charles Manson. So just consider him like an honorable-mention serial killer, because he sucked.

Committed AF

CHAPTER 5

Basic Breakups

If there's one thing that unites us all in basicness, it's breakups. Even if you've never been the dumpee and you are a serial dumper, it hurts (unless you're a sadist, and I've def dated a few of those). Women love to bond over breakups, usually after midnight in the bathroom at a club or bar, when we're wasted and on the verge of drunk-texting the exact ex we are bitching about. I mean, the odds of me going into a public bathroom at night and not hearing two girls chat about fuckboys are slim. I've talked to total strangers in the bathroom about my deepest, darkest feelings after a breakup. From the bathrooms at Les Deux to Goa to Hyde (ah, those were the days; twenty-one years old and carefree AF), I have bonded with people over a breakup. It's like a rite of passage or a cultural phenomenon, and it is basic AF. I'm thirty and it's *still* happening. I bet ninety-year-old women in nursing homes are still talking about this shit. It never ends.

As for me, I've had some pretty public breakups. From Jax to Patrick to the guy who tried to sell a sex tape of me to TMZ, I've had people I have never met gossiping and tweeting about what happened to my relationships, which is pretty weird. Because it's so public, people on social media are always asking me how I get over breakups—or how to get over their own. It's the number one topic I get asked about. Like this question:

"I'm in a toxic on-and-off relationship and we fight all the time. How do you know when to call it quits?"

Or this:

"What are the top things that should be nonnegotiable in a relationship? Or top things that make a healthy relationship?"

Or this:

"What's the best way to meet a boyfriend? Friends? Apps? Work? Bars?"

But while it's universal and it's basic to sit around and bond over breakups, we all deal with them differently. And I am no relationship expert or breakup guru, even though I feel like some of my breakups have been pretty extreme, so I've learned some solid lessons from them. Take Jax. He cheated on me, so I retaliated by changing his Twitter handle to "Mrs. Stassi Schroeder" (it was easy to figure out his password because guys are lazy AF and pick passwords like 123456). After the Twitter sabotage, I keyed his car. I have legit keyed a few cars in my life as revenge after a breakup. I actually keyed one boyfriend's car *right in front of him*, and he ended up trying to sue me but I was broke at the time, so every time he'd call and try to get a confession out of me I'd just lie. I mean, he's the one who cheated, right? Plus, I was drunk when I keyed his car, obviously. No one is out there soberly keying cars to get even after a breakup.

Before we started filming the first season of *Vanderpump Rules*, I said that my worst nightmare would be to go through a breakup on camera. I actually knew that Jax and I weren't going to work out, but I promised myself that I would just stay with him until filming was over to spare myself the humiliation. That is until a week into filming. I found out off camera one morning that Jax had cheated on me and might have gotten a girl pregnant in Vegas. I immediately started texting him and all my friends. I was sobbing, hyperventilating, and literally throwing up in my toilet. On the show, there is a scene where Katie, Kristen, and some other friends all come over and we end up drinking Jax's Cristal champagne ($200 champs!!)

out of Solo cups. That was one of the most intense scenes I've ever filmed because the scene was never supposed to happen. I was not even scheduled to film that day. I was sitting there, no makeup on, in my pj's, sobbing—and the producers must have found out what was happening because all of a sudden they came bursting through my door with the camera crew! At first I was furious, but then I quickly realized that I had signed up for this. I dare anyone to try to say this show is scripted. It couldn't be more real.

Next there were the Patrick breakup(s), which were beyond bad. We were always on-again, off-again, and for a long time he refused to go on *Vanderpump* and would say things like, "I could never be with someone who would do a show like that." So like an idiot I quit the show for a while and gave up my job and my friends for him. After a while during one of our off periods I was like, "I just tossed my job and friends aside for you and I'm still miserable! I am going back to the show and getting my life back and my friends back." And I did. Eventually he agreed to go on the show and he did like five episodes, which are hard for me to watch now because it's like I was brainwashed and didn't know how to stick up for myself. Like I couldn't even form sentences because I was walking on eggshells all the time. You'd think he would have been on his best behavior on camera and that it would be easy not to be a condescending prick for a few minutes, but he managed to look like an asshole every single time. It's pretty amazing.

I was too far in it to realize his full degree of assholeness, and so as a thank-you for going on the show I booked a Mexican vacation for our four-year anniversary. But like I already told you, he broke up with me *on* our anniversary, so I went to Mexico with my friends instead and I cried, drank piña coladas, and took Xanax, so I don't remember a lot of the vacation. I didn't key his car when I got back, but I did get into Patrick's Twitter account to revoke his "verified" status by changing his Twitter handle. Sadly, Patrick managed to get his status reinstated. When you find yourself wanting to know someone's password, you know you're about to go down a deep dark rabbit hole, so I never want to go to that place again. Plus, it gives them reason to blame *you* even though they fucked up. Like after Jax and I broke up, his guy friends would defend him and I would be like, "He cheated on me!" And they would say, "But you changed his Twitter handle!" Like it's the same thing. So basically you lose in the end.

The worst breakup advice I've ever heard is "get even," because it can sometimes land you in jail, let's be real. Keying a car maybe felt good in the moment, but it just made me feel pathetic the next day, so it was totes not worth it. I wanted to get even with the guy who tried to sell the sex tape of me, because it was one of the scariest things that has ever happened to me. I found out about it the day I moved to New York City, in 2014. The plane landed and I had text messages from Lisa Vanderpump and our producer Alex Baskin saying *Call me 911*. My heart literally fell into my asshole (I'm sure that's medically possible, because I felt it), and when I found out this ex was trying to sell TMZ a tape of me masturbating, I fell on the floor of JFK crying. People probably thought I was losing my mind, which I kind of was. For real, it was one of the most frightening things that's ever happened to me (much scarier than doors slamming in the Los Feliz murder house). My agent and lawyer told me to ignore the guy and to not say anything about it on social media, but he started showing up at my old apartment and scaring my ex-roommate. Then he asked Lisa Vanderpump for $900 to *not* release the tape, and I was like, *$900?? That's all I'm worth?!* What kind of amateur extortionist only asks for $900? But he got his money, and I never heard from him again.

So like I said, I am not a breakup expert, but I have learned a few basic lessons over the years that might help if you find yourself pouring your heart out to a total stranger about your breakup at midnight in a public bathroom, or wanting to smash the windshield of someone's car with a baseball bat like Beyoncé because they cheated on you, or having a meltdown in JFK because a crazy ex is trying to sell a gossip site a tape of you masturbating. You know, normal breakup stuff. So to help you avoid some of these pitfalls, here are a few ways I've learned to cope over the years (that are healthier than vandalism or social media revenge).

Next Level Basic Tips:
HOW TO MOVE ON FROM A BREAKUP

ALLOW YOURSELF TO FREAKING FEEL IT

The best breakup advice I've ever gotten is to let yourself feel your feelings. Basically I cry a fuck-ton, and feel really, really sorry for myself for as long as it takes to move on (in my case, usually a few weeks). I also surround myself with friends but then demand they go home at a decent hour so I can cry again all by myself and let it all out. I hate it when people tell you to "buck up" when what you really need to do is wallow and hard-core mourn and become a degenerate for a while. It helps, and it's healthy. So I say wallow if you wanna.

HIRE A BREAKUP NANNY

After my breakup with Patrick, I literally paid my childhood friend Alex Stafford to come stay with me and take care of me like a nurse-caretaker-babysitter-therapist. She is legit a saint—Saint Alex—because she took care of my dogs, paid my bills, cleaned my place, took my car to the shop, let me sleep until noon, and then woke me up with a Diet Dr Pepper in hand and let me watch whatever cheesy movies I wanted to watch. *And* she fed me—sometimes literally putting food into my mouth as if I were a big, brokenhearted, pizza-eating baby. I was like Mariah

Carey on crack, and she was my most loyal diligent assistant. It worked out for Alex, not just because I paid her but because she ended up loving Los Angeles so much she stayed and now she lives a few blocks away from me. She deserves to be canonized, or at least to have this book dedicated to her.

GET OUT OF TOWN

Once I get out of the breakup-nanny phase (usually after a few weeks), it's time to get back in the saddle, and a great way to do this is to plan a girls' trip. It can be for two nights or a week, out of the country or an hour away. It helps get your mind off things and reminds you that your friends are way more important than some bro who is too lazy to think of a decent Twitter password.

GET BASIC AF

Breakups unite us in basicness, and there's nothing more basic than girls' nights and a breakup makeover. All of a sudden we want to throw on a bandage dress and push-up bra, get a mani-pedi (bright red is a good basic post-breakup pick) and a blowout, and post hot photos of ourselves online. My early twenties was my most embarrassing dating era, and after a breakup I would ask friends to post hot photos of me online and comment things like, *OMG, I can't believe that guy last night*, even though I might have only talked to some random dude for like two minutes. When you're getting basic after a breakup, the Snapchat pretty filter is your BFF, and you start reading female-empowerment books like this one. If filtering the shit out of your photos helps you move on, I say do it.

(DRUNK) RETAIL THERAPY

It's a good sign when you've moved on from a breakup and you start talking to new dudes, but if those new dudes start ghosting you, that's when it's time to go to the Neiman's bar (or any bar that has easy access to shopping) to get wasted. I go straight to the Beverly Hills Neiman's top-floor bar and order an espresso martini because it gets me wasted but also keeps me awake while I shop. They give you an extra shaker, so it's like you're getting three martinis for the price of one. I also order the off-the-menu three-scoop salad, which is tuna salad, egg salad, and chicken salad, because it makes me feel like I'm being skinny and not eating my feelings (which I totes am). Then I head straight to the shoe section—my fave—and shop until I block out any memory of the person who just broke up with me.

BUY YOURSELF A BREAKUP PRESENT

Drunk shoe shopping at Neiman's is one thing (and it helps), but buying yourself a legit breakup gift makes you feel like a baller and reminds you that you don't need a man to buy jewelry or flowers or gifts for you, because you are a badass. After Jax and I broke up I took his credit card and bought myself a bracelet from J.Crew, even though I could have bought a much nicer bracelet with my own credit card, thanks very much. After Patrick and I broke up (the first time, for six months) I designed a ring with the jewelry designer Kyle Chan. Patrick broke up with me like every four days, but after the final *real* breakup I splurged and bought myself a vintage gold Cartier watch—and it made me feel much better. Still does.

So maybe the next time you get ghosted or dumped by some dude, you'll hire a friend to coddle you and feed you pizza, or you'll buy yourself a vintage watch and realize that *you do not need that asshole*! And remember that getting even and keying cars or committing social media crimes never, ever works and only makes you feel crappy and pathetic in the end. That said, there is one person that I still fantasize about getting even with and that's you, FRANK, the one who tried to sell the sex tape of me to TMZ. I won't do anything drastic to get back at FRANK because that would be totally pathetic and sad, but I think saying his name is pretty good payback so whatevs . . . FRANK.

Next Level Basic TAKEAWAY

When it comes to getting through a breakup, as long as you're not hurting anyone, do whatever you have to do to feel your feelings and *move on*. Don't be embarrassed to cry, drink wine, and watch Lifetime movies for two days straight! If you need to build a creepy shrine to your ex with photos and pieces of clothing they left at your place *do it*. And if you then need to burn all those photos and clothes in the sink, do that too (safely). I've figured out what works for me (breakup nannies, shopping, drinking), so your job is to discover your own personal version of a breakup nanny and make that your prescription for getting through this shit. Sometimes it'll take two weeks, and sometimes it'll take two months, but I promise, if you stick to what you know works, no matter how ridiculous it is, you'll get there.

CHAPTER 6

Next Level Dealbreakers

ecause of *Vanderpump*, my love life has been out there on full display for the world to see (and to Twitter-shame—thanks guys!). Based on my on-camera history, you might not think I have too many dealbreakers, since I did date a cheater and that *should* be like dealbreaker #1 (besides being a serial killer, obvi). But you live and learn, and what I've learned is that everyone has dealbreakers, and they can sometimes be weird and basic AF. And sometimes they change, like if you meet a super-hot serial killer who looks like Tom Hardy because . . . YOLO.

Sometimes things become dealbreakers because a psycho ex had a certain habit or trait and once you break up you vow never to date a person who eats their pizza with a knife and fork/loves jazz/wears fedoras. For example, if you've watched *Vanderpump Rules* you might know that I've dated a few guys who have what *some* people might consider serious dealbreakers. Things like:

▶ Maybe getting a girl pregnant in Vegas while you're still dating. (Hi, Jax!)

▶ Getting arrested in Hawaii for stealing sunglasses. (Jax again.)

▶ Wearing chunky knit sweaters in the middle of summer *and* getting three nose jobs. (You guessed it: Jax.)

▶ Trying to sell a sex tape of you. (FRANK.)

▶ Condescendingly talking to you by using "fancy" words to try to trip you up, like "myopic," "juggernaut," or "galvanize." (Thanks, Patrick.)

▶ Getting *Game of Thrones* references wrong. (Patrick's second offense.)

▶ Not knowing the difference between Cholula and sriracha. (#Patrick.)

So to celebrate the fact that we all have (or should have) some pretty personal dealbreakers (which we break because: we're human), I'm going to share mine with you. I'm not doing this because I think you need to adopt my own personal dealbreakers and become a clone of me. Please. I'm doing it so that you can feel a little less ashamed of your own ridiculous dealbreakers. If you don't have any, I suggest you make a list like this now so that you don't end up dating a cheater who hates animals and hot sauce and loves silent discos or Dubsmashing. Y'all can do better than *that*.

Top Twelve Ultimate Dealbreakers

1. PEOPLE WHO ARE RUDE TO SERVERS

This is a legit dealbreaker for me, maybe from all those years working at Sur. Or maybe because it's just basic fucking human decency to treat servers with respect. This is not one I'm willing to make exceptions for. I don't care if Chris Hemsworth pulls out the Hope diamond to propose to me and then tells a waiter to "fuck off, my soup is cold!" I would say no and walk away (but maybe I would take the diamond with me). Being rude to servers should honestly be up there with mass murder. There is never an excuse for this, unless, like, you witness your server spitting in your food or something, in which case, proceed with the rudeness.

2. DUBSMASHERS

Yeah, that little app that allows you to mouth the words of different movie scenes. I don't know why this bothers me so much—maybe because I rarely see a funny one, and when people post lame Dubsmashes, it kind of feels like a reflection of their underdeveloped sense of humor.

3. MALE GYM SELFIES

We get it, guys, you work out. Women can get away with this, but there is something about a male gym selfie that really irks me to my basic-ass core. It's the douche level, you know what I mean? When I was dating Jax Taylor and hacking into his social media accounts, I would delete his gym selfies. That was fun. If you are in the market for a little revenge and your ex posts gym selfies, it *can* be cathartic to delete them, *but* I am not condoning social-media crimes, so maybe don't follow my lead here. Oh, and PS—posting your cross-training workout stats is basically equivalent to a gym selfie, whether you're male or female. No. One. Cares. Plus—you're doing a cross-training workout in an air-conditioned gym, you're not trekking the Himalayas barefoot.

4. PEOPLE WHO DON'T CHARGE THEIR PHONES

I can't stress this enough. It's pretty much the easiest thing in the world to plug a phone into a charger, and the benefits of that action are supreme. I've contemplated cutting some people out of my life because of their low phone charge. But then I realized that I'd be left with no friends, so . . . People with uncharged phones deserve to be weeded out of existence. It's just basic evolution. Survival of the fittest, guys. I don't care how "busy" you are or how drunk you get. It's the twenty-first century—find a charger.

5. CAT PEOPLE

CATS ARE TRYING TO KILL YOU, PEOPLE. Google it. For realzies. They aren't very nice; they never get excited to see their owner; they make the house smell like piss. I don't get it. They are cute though, I'll give you that. But I could never date a true cat lover. I would rather die.

6. PEOPLE WHO LOVE NATURE

Listen, I love a pretty day outside. I love sunshine, the beach, maybe a mountain or two (as long as I don't have to scale it). But to me, a brisk fall walk in Manhattan to Saks sounds like a good way to get some nature in. There is a difference between appreciating nature and then being so obsessed that the first date you ask someone on is to go hiking up Runyon Canyon with a green juice in hand for hydration or whatever. I would never go on that first date. And

I could never really love someone who wanted to, like, meditate in a forest. Gross.

7. TRIBAL TATTOOS

I think I'd rather tattoo "Hidden Valley Ranch" on my forehead than get a tribal tattoo anywhere on my body. I might even date someone with "Hidden Valley Ranch" tattooed on their forehead over someone with a tribal tattoo on their bicep. I feel like this is self-explanatory.

8. PEOPLE WHO USE SIRI IN PUBLIC

There's a special place in hell for people who use Siri to text/take notes in public. First, it's confusing to every other pedestrian walking by. I always wonder, "Wait, is this person talking to *me*?" It's rude AF to put that burden on a stranger. Second, if you do this you risk looking like someone who just pleaded insanity in a murder trial and then fled with their phone. Finally, my boyfriend, Beau, does this in public, so I have broken my own rule.

9. PEOPLE WHO SAY, "CAN I PICK YOUR BRAIN?"

The obvious answer to this question is "Um, no." What's wrong with saying, "Can you give me advice?" There's not one positive thing about this phrase, and if someone said it to me on a first date I would probably pretend to go to the bathroom and just bolt. There are SO MANY OTHER THINGS YOU CAN SAY instead of this icky phrase. I mean, think about the mental image this conjures up. No, thanks.

10. PEOPLE WHO BRAG ABOUT NOT OWNING A TV

Please. You think it's cool or edgy to stare at the walls all day and night? There are no studies that show that watching TV makes you dumber, and it definitely makes you less cool. And how could you *not* want to watch *Game of Thrones* or *The Walking Dead*? What is wrong with you? It's not that people choose not to watch TV that bothers me the most—it's that they *brag* about not watching TV like it's such an accomplishment. Plus they usually tack on something about the fact that they read books instead of watching TV and it's like, excuse me, I am capable of watching the Kardashi-ans *and* reading books. They're not mutually exclusive activities. Just go live in the same town as people who love nature and stop trying to convert the rest of us to your "no TV" lifestyle. Plus, we all know you're secretly watching Netflix on your phone!

11. PEOPLE WHO REFUSE TO SHARE THE NAME OF THEIR HOUSEKEEPER

This is so selfish. I mean, are they cleaning your place all day and night 365 days a year? I don't think so, so give me their number. I realize this might be an LA thing, coveting other people's housekeepers. But the point is—it's a thing!

12. PEOPLE WHO JUDGE WHEN YOU ORDER A DRINK BEFORE NOON

If I went on a date to an all-day pool party that started at 10:00 a.m. and my date scolded me for having a cocktail, I would *know* he wasn't "the one." In fact, in that moment he would become my mortal enemy.

Now that I've laid out my absolute dealbreakers, you should know that my boyfriend Dubsmashes. He also doesn't charge his phone. Oh, and he doesn't *hate* cats and believe they're put on this earth to steal our souls like I do. But I'm still with him. So I guess you know that if someone has one or more of your Next Level Basic dealbreakers and you don't ghost them right there on the spot, it's the real deal.

Next Level Basic TAKEAWAY

It's taken me more than a decade to compile my list of dealbreakers—and in another decade the list might be totally different. Like, I may be open to cat people (kill me), and I might marry a Dubsmasher (it's possible). What I've learned from having dealbreakers is that it helps you get focused, not just on what you do really want out of a relationship—but on what you *don't* want. It helps you have standards, no matter how basic they might be.

CHARGED UP

You're probably getting the message that I can be weird and basic AF. So you may as well know that one of my "quirks" is that I cannot associate with anyone who doesn't have their phone fully charged at all times. I mean, that's *sort of* an exaggeration, but not totally. I might not walk out on you in the middle of dinner, but I will silently judge you and wonder whether you were raised by a crazed maniac in the woods with no cell reception, portable chargers, or outlets to plug your phone into.

If you truly want to become Next Level Basic, you need to make sure you're not one of those people who are like, "Oh, I didn't get your text because my phone died." Or, "Oh, we have to sit here for twenty minutes so I can charge my phone because it's at 2 percent, so we'll be late for the movie because I AM A PSYCHO."

Do I silently (or loudly) judge people when I notice their phone charges are getting low? Hell yes. How hard is it to plug your phone in overnight, or carry around a charger, or have a charging case? Look at your phone right now. I am judging you right this minute. That said, it's not like I'm a perfect human who walks around with my phone at 100 percent charge all the time. I have spent some time psychoanalyzing myself to try to figure out why losing charge gives me such anxiety, and it comes from a deep fear of finding myself in a situation where I can't share an Instagram story or post. Like, what if

I run into Joaquin Phoenix and in that very moment my phone goes dead? It's very stressful.

So to help you (or me) get over this issue, I have created a chart that will show you why you need to charge that shit and up your game if you're truly a basic bitch. Or if you want me to not hate you.

100 PERCENT

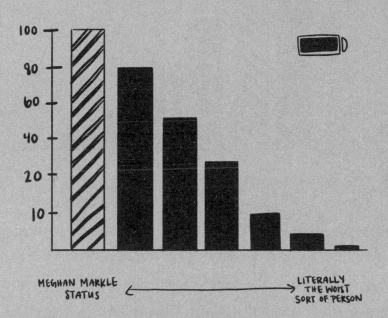

Basically, you deserve everything Meghan Markle got, without the weird royal rules (like why the eff isn't she allowed to eat shellfish, or wear colored nail polish?). Ugh, that would kill me. Anyhow . . . You 100 percent (pun intended) deserve some sort of royal title . . . duchess, duke, princess, queen, king, viscountess . . . but without any annoying responsibilities, of course. And you can eat shellfish all day long if you want, and paint your nails hot pink.

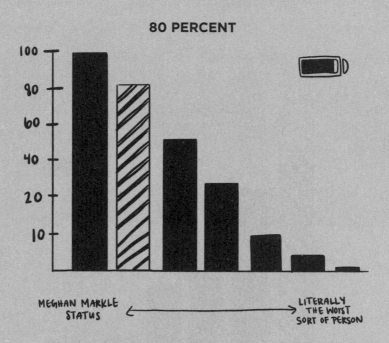

80 PERCENT

MEGHAN MARKLE STATUS ← → LITERALLY THE WORST SORT OF PERSON

I'm worried about you, but I'm still going to have your back and make up some sort of excuse as to why your phone is about to go to 79 percent. I realize that 80 percent still does seem high and you are probably asking yourself why I'm not rewarding you in some way. (Rewards are reserved for people who have battery chargers as their phone cases and who also carry portable power chargers in their handbags, so don't go patting yourself on the back.) But this is tough love, and I can't fully get behind you if you don't respect yourself enough to stay fully charged. I won't hate you, but I won't applaud you either.

50 PERCENT

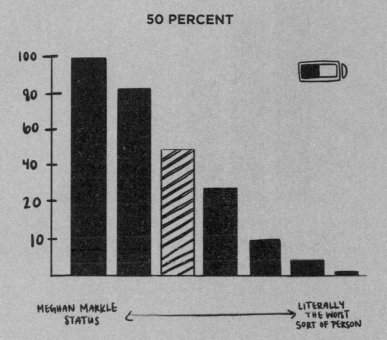

MEGHAN MARKLE STATUS ← → LITERALLY THE WORST SORT OF PERSON

You should probably start wondering where you went wrong in life. Maybe you partied a little too much in your twenties? Maybe you didn't pay attention enough in school? Maybe there was some weird butterfly-effect thing that caused you to be a 50-percent-charged type of person. Whatever it is, it's time to seek help and do the work to really figure yourself out. I wish you luck.

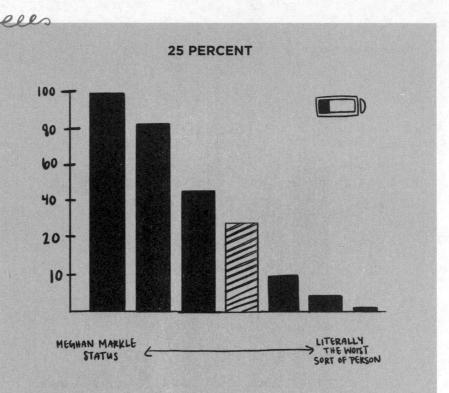

25 PERCENT

MEGHAN MARKLE STATUS ← → LITERALLY THE WORST SORT OF PERSON

You most definitely aren't a functioning citizen, and you are also definitely not contributing to the world in any meaningful way. I bet you don't like puppies. In fact, I bet puppies don't even like *you*. Charge your phone!

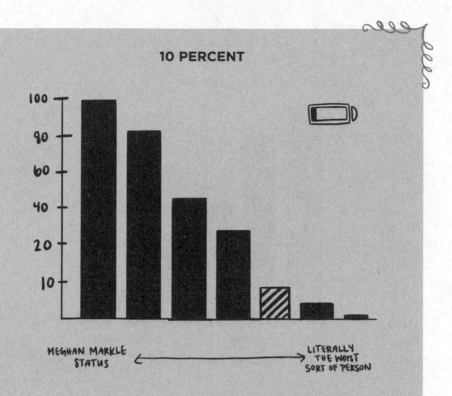

10 PERCENT

MEGHAN MARKLE STATUS ← → LITERALLY THE WORST SORT OF PERSON

You have definitely committed a murder before. I saw a meme on Instagram (basic AF, I'm aware), and it read, "The average person walks past a murderer thirty-six times in their life." Um, *what*? So if there are that many murderers out there, to the point where each of us are going to eventually see thirty-six of them (or one murderer thirty-six times), then you 10-percent-battery-charge people are definitely part of that group. You guys! Stop murdering and just charge your freakin' phones. Get your priorities in line. It's not that hard.

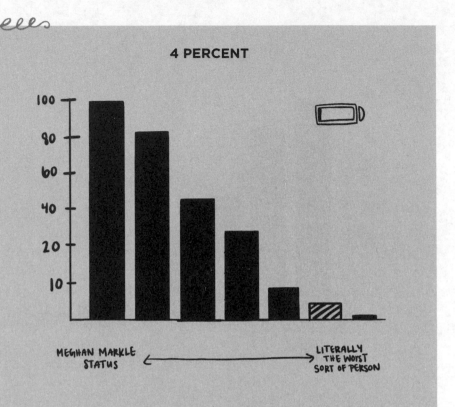

4 PERCENT

MEGHAN MARKLE STATUS ← → LITERALLY THE WORST SORT OF PERSON

We are now way past single-murderer types. You have multiple killings under your belt. You may even have a family that you kidnapped living under your house in a basement and your roommates just haven't noticed because they're busy being functioning adults charging their phones. You, my friend, are a serial killer.

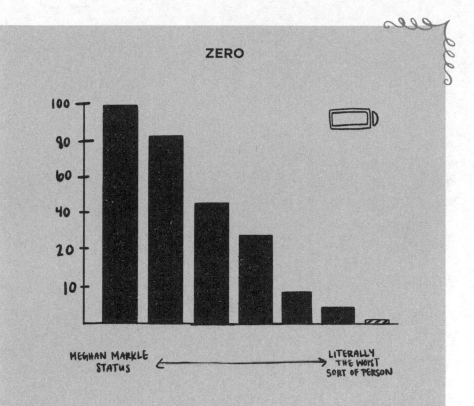

ZERO

MEGHAN MARKLE STATUS ⟵⟶ LITERALLY THE WORST SORT OF PERSON

You are now part of the percentage of people who should be weeded out of the world. Even if I got it all wrong and you haven't murdered anyone, overpopulation is still a thing, and you have *gots* to go. May you (and your uncharged phone) rest in peace.

CHAPTER 7

Like a Virgin

Losing your virginity is one of the most basic rites of passage we all go through. But before it happens, we obsess about it, fear it, or both. Usually both.

I never had a plan for myself in terms of losing my virginity. I remember the first few times as a kid where I became aware that I got a tingly feeling "down there." I didn't know what it meant or what it was but I knew something funny happened every time I watched *Dirty Dancing* and *Pretty Woman*. I remember being around six or seven and I would secretly fast-forward to the part in *Dirty Dancing* where Baby and Johnny finally took their dancing to the, um, next level, and that part in *Pretty Woman* where Richard Gere and Julia Roberts get going on a piano in the mid-

dle of a hotel ballroom. (Now that I think of it, it's like the most unrealistic thing ever . . . They just order a bunch of people to leave a public place and everyone actually listens and gets up without question so those two can just bang it out on a hotel piano?!) If anything has created a disconnect between real sex and fantasy sex, it's rom-coms.

As I got older, I graduated from getting off to *Dirty Dancing* to more sophisticated porn like *Inventing the Abbotts* (hello, young Joaquin Phoenix) or *9½ Weeks*. As a preteen, I took to *Cosmopolitan* magazine, and I would secretly stay up and read the excerpts of romance novels that they always had at the end of each issue. Once I got my license and had the freedom to do what I wanted, I drove my ass to Barnes & Noble and bought those books I had read the excerpts of in *Cosmo*. But with all this preoccupation with my sexuality, I never had an idea of what I wanted my "first time" to be like. I knew I didn't like high school boys because I always felt way more mature than them, so going on dates with someone my own age bored me. Despite what you might think from watching *Vanderpump*, I didn't even make out with anyone until I was sixteen. Very few people can say their "losing my virginity" story is totally epic, and for most of us (like me), the actual event was basic AF. All I knew about losing my virginity was that it was going to be with a man, not a boy. And I most definitely accomplished that. And it was mortifying. I'm cringing and sweating even thinking about it right now.

Clichéd enough, I lost my virginity on prom night . . . only I didn't go to prom. I had a lot of friends who were older than I was, and my parents were the type of parents who really trusted me and gave me the freedom to do what I wanted. I rarely had a curfew, and if I did, I probably came home before expected. Because I had so much freedom, I never wanted to rebel. I made straight A's, I never did anything that would get me grounded—I was pretty boring, TBH. So when my older friends asked me to join them on a trip to Chicago, on the last weekend of my senior year in high school, my parents let me go. (Yes, I was going to miss my senior prom, but as I've mentioned, I was *supes* uninterested in normal teenage stuff.)

The first night in Chicago, I realized that we were hanging out with a guy I'd had a major crush on—a guy who was twenty-seven years old (aka a *man*). He legit looked like Matthew McConaughey, like a total doppelgänger, so for the sake of this conversation let's just call this man Matt. So we all go out (I had a fake ID, obvs). Later, a big group of us go back to his place. I flirted with him as much as I could, having no idea if he would take someone like me seriously. Being the seventeen-year-old rookie that I was, I realized I was drunk and tired, and so I went into his room. Next thing I know, he comes in the room and lies next to me on the bed. My inner geeky-weirdo-who-always-knew-she-wanted-to-lose-her-virginity-to-an-actual-man self starts freaking out (in a good way). And then he turns to me and says, "Stassi, are you eighteen?" *HOLY SHIT. HOLY SHIT.*

HOLY SHIT. (That was my inner thought process, FYI.) At that very moment, I knew that I had two paths in front of me. I either tell him the truth (I was seventeen), or I could lie and YOLO it. And I obviously YOLO'd the shit out of it. (Listen, before you judge me, I was only one month away from turning eighteen, and mentally I felt like I was about twenty-six, so, like, let's split the difference.)

We start making out . . . and this is where the cringing really begins. So, like I said, I had no idea what to do when it came to sex or making out, and that included grooming. Yes, ladies and gents—I had a full-blown bush. I had hoped this guy would make out with me, but I never imagined anything would happen involving my vagina! Honestly, props to him for staying down there so long. I know some guys are into that, so maybe he was just one of them. Next, he takes off his pants and asks me if this is okay, to which I said yes. Mind you, he was not aware that I was a virgin. Now that I'm reliving this totally embarrassing moment for you, I'm very appreciative of his asking me if what he was doing was okay every step of the way. So we did it, and it hurt like hell. I'm pretty much just lying there because I'M A VIRGIN AND VIRGINS HAVE NO CLUE WHAT TO DO. After a few minutes, I panicked and realized I was way out of my league. Did I sexily roll away like some diva to end the session? No. I . . . closed my eyes and pretended to pass out. Yep, like Amy Schumer in *Trainwreck*, I legit just put my head to the side and pretended to sleep. So he stopped. Then *he* fell asleep. Just like in *9½ Weeks*.

I woke up the next morning to all his "bros" coming in the room asking us if we had a good night (in the douchiest frat-boy way possible). I'm mortified all over again—it's bright as shit in this room, my makeup is all over my face, I just lost my virginity *and* I'm naked in a man's bed with a full bush. Matt tells them to get out of the room, he again asks if I'm okay, and then he says he's going to take a shower. I realized it was my opportunity to flee and get a cab, so I started doing some *Mission Impossible* shit in my brain to plan my escape. I quickly got up and got dressed, but when I turned to look at the bed, there was a bloodstain.

My heart sank into my vagina (also totally medically possible). I panicked and found a tiny mini pillow (I'm talking like six-by-six pincushion-type pillow), and I just put it right on the bloodstain. What was I thinking? Like the mini pillow was some Harry Potter invisibility cloak that would hide it from this guy forever? The pillow only drew more attention to it, but I wasn't staying around to find out how Matt would make the big discovery. Damn that mini pillow! So, yep. I ran off. And that is the basic AF way that I lost my virginity. I have seen Matt a few times since then, and we never talked about our night of passionate sex (aka passing out), but my 2006 vagina bush and that mini pillow will haunt me forever.

Let me be the first to say that I am no sexual expert. Any advice or tips I pass along are based purely on my own experiences being a thirty-year-old woman who has been having sex for the last thirteen years of her life. I love sex (especially with the right person), I go through phases with porn, I masturbate, I've never done anal (seems painful), I've been with around fifteen people, I've waxed, I've shaved, I've had a finger up my ass (didn't like it), I'm a huge fan of cunnilingus, I've worn lingerie, I've queefed (come on, it happens to all of us), I've gone through dry spells, I've never had a one-night stand, and I love a good vibrator. See? Average thirty-year-old sexually-active woman.

As a nonexpert who happens to have thirteen years of experience under my (garter) belt, here are just a few things to pass along so that you're prepared when you get to *that moment*, whether it's the first moment or the five hundredth.

Next Level Basic SEX TIPS

LESSON #1

My "losing my virginity" story taught me some basic grooming lessons. Now I realize we all like different things (like maybe you prefer that seventies Chewbacca bush), but I personally like to be completely hairless. Whether it's a wax or shave, I want it off. There's no way I could feel my hottest self with hair down there. But this is about what makes *you* feel best. So if rocking a fro down there makes you feel sexy, *do it*. Just make sure your nether region is always the way *you* want it to look.

LESSON #2

I recently had my vagina vajazzled with glitter. Yes, you read that right. I went in for a normal wax and discovered that you can actually use stencils to glitter your little flower. I love anything sparkly, so obviously the idea of a sparkly vagina fed my soul in a profound way. Needless to say, I came home with lots of silver and gold stars down there. (I chose neutral metallics, as I wanted them to match my outfits.) It was so extra, and I loved it. Totes recommend. And just know that you don't *have* to do this to have great sex, since I understand that not everyone wants a disco vagina. But if there is something that makes *you* feel sexy and it's a little unconventional—go for it.

LESSON #3

This might sound weird, but if you're a single girl who is going on dates or open to "hooking up" with someone on random nights, carry an extra pair of cute undies with you at all times. If you think something is about to go down, run (or casually walk, which is sexier than running) to the restroom and switch out your undies for a new pair and just toss the old. They'll never know, and you'll feel like Julia Roberts in *Pretty Woman* when Richard Gere tells everyone to get out of the room so he can bang her.

LESSON #4

In my experience, sex gets better as I get to know someone. The first time is never the best time because I have zero idea what that person is into, so I get too in my head. I vote to never judge the first few times you sleep with someone. Don't give up on the guy/girl if it isn't the absolute best right away. Everyone wants to have that "meant for each other" perfect night of sex the first time. That shit rarely happens. Sex ain't a Disney movie, y'all. You're not slutty Cinderella, so be patient.

LESSON #5

I can't stand "when to give it up" rules. You're not giving anything up. You are actively participating in a fun act with another human being. So actively participate whenever you want to, whether it's the first date, fortieth date, or if you haven't even had a date at all. You do you.

LESSON #6

Every single person has body insecurities. Recognizing that will set you free. I've never had abs. Actually I've never even had one ab, not even at the age of two. If I thought about that during sex, I would never be able to enjoy myself, much less orgasm. Letting your insecurities go is the most important sex advice I feel I could ever express, so there you go. Rock your non-ab abs or your untight ass like you're the hottest human to ever walk the planet—which you are, BTW.

Next Level Basic TAKEAWAY

When it comes to losing our virginity, we are all basic AF. I don't care if you've read every book on sex and watched every porn out there (which isn't a great place to get sex advice anyway, IMHO), when you first start out, you are like a newborn baby learning to walk. The biggest thing I've learned over the years is that confidence—not trying to be perfect—is the key to great sex.

VANDERPUMP RULES
HOOKUP FLOW CHART

Peter ~~~~ Katie ～～～ Tom Schwartz

Stassi

Beau   Carter

Tom Sandoval

Jax ~~~~ Kristen   Ariana

James

Brittany   Lala

—————— dating
～～～～ engaged/married
~~~~~~ fling/hooked up/made out

CHAPTER 8

Witches of WeHo

Witch [noun]: A woman who is believed to have magical powers and, especially in stories, uses them to help or harm people.

I think people who watch *Vanderpump* have an impression of me as not just a basic bitch but a bitch bitch. Nothing is further from the truth (well, maybe *some* things). I have always been a girl's girl, and now I'm a woman's woman, I guess (hello, thirty!). I have plenty of male friends, but for the most part my closest friends are female, and I love being around other women. Sure, I can be blunt (sometimes in a controversial way, so there's that), but I love my friends and would do anything for them. We've been called the "Witches of WeHo," and we wear that title with pride. I mean, witches are women who stick together and have magical powers, right? I'm 100 percent cool with that.

There *is* one witchy friendship-related rumor that started because of *Vanderpump* that drives me crazy, so I'd like to set the record straight right here, right now. And that rumor is that I have an "A" group of friends and a "B" group of friends. So if my "A" group (I guess like the alpha group) pisses me off, I can slum it and hang out with my "B" group (like friend stand-ins or extras or something). People actually think I rank my friends and have it all planned out so that I'm never alone and friendless. Please!

The rumor started because in season one of *Vanderpump* we went to Vegas for my birthday. Kristen and Katie are my friends *and* cast members, so of course they were coming, but I asked the producers if I could invite some non-cast-member friends too, but these other friends could only come Saturday because they had to work at Sur on Friday. Friday night in Vegas I got in a huge fight with Kristen and Katie because my ex Jax showed up uninvited to dinner and caused a major fight that had all my friends siding with him. The next day my "other" friends showed up (*because they had to work Friday, not because I'm a basic, evil witch!*), and I made a joke on camera about the fact that I was pissed at my "A friends," so my "B friends" were coming to hang out with me, as if they were my little minions or something. So I guess what happens in Vegas does *not* stay in Vegas, and what you say on camera STAYS IN PEOPLE'S MINDS FOREVER.

I cringe every time I watch that interview, even though I thought it was funny in the moment. In fact, I'm cringing right now, and I feel like I should send a text to that supposed "B" crew again and apologize, even though I did nothing wrong but make a joke on camera! Because of the show, people come up to me all the time and say they think I'm going to be an asshole just for the sake of it. I think people expect me to be a mean girl because in season one I just went full-blown cray. I was like a bat out of hell and did not give an eff. If I *am* mean or bitchy it's because someone *deserves it*! Just kidding. Sort of. It's actually because they have hurt me or one of my friends and I maybe get a little vengeful. I mean, there is an element of truth to the fact that I am not warm and fuzzy BFFs with every person who crosses my path. You have to earn your place in my life, just like I think I have to earn my place in *your* life. It just takes a while to be my best friend and commit to that friendship, and I'm not going to pretend to like you if I think you're full of BS. That's pretty basic, right?

People always say about *Vanderpump*, "You're just friends with these people for a story line." But what makes *Vanderpump* work is that we are an actual group of friends and we take our friendship very seriously. Okay, sure, my best friend Kristen had sex with my ex and we didn't speak for a year and a half, but once we had that time apart we cared enough to rebuild our friendship, and now it's even stronger. I mean, how many people stay best friends with the person who slept with their ex?! I feel like we deserve some sort of medal. Same with Katie. We grew apart for a while, like friends sometimes do, but when we came back together that "time-out" made us understand each other on a deeper level. On the other hand, sometimes you do need to cut people out of your life if it's toxic and causing you more stress than happiness, but the true ride-or-die besties are there for life.

On *Vanderpump* (and IRL), Scheana Shay and I have had a frenemies kind of bond. I honestly really admire Scheana for her basicness. She uses the pretty/flower/animal filter on every-thing, she only takes photos on one side of her face, she does the duck face in every photo, and she thinks being called a "bootleg Kardashian" is a compliment. Think I'm throwing shade? Hell no. That girl be living her best life. The frenemy relationship is complicated, and if you give them time to blossom (instead of wilt into a toxic hell of fights and backstabbing) they might just turn into the real deal.

Whether they're frenemies or BFFs, I don't understand or trust women who have *no* female friends. I mean, girlfriends enhance your life and make it more sparkly and glittery and brighter, like a freakin' rhinestone Louboutin. Plus, women are so strong and multifaceted. Bros keep it pretty surface-level for the most part, but with women we want to uncover and discover and work through things, and I love that connection. Let's just be real—women are just so much more interesting than men.

My friends have gotten me through everything. I can call

them at three or four in the morning and I know someone will drive over if I need them to dry my tears or pour me some wine and let me listen to *Les Mis* on repeat. When I think of my life and where I've been blessed, I've been #BLESSED in the friends department, and I feel thankful for that. When you find real friends you work through shit and forgive and forget. And that's how I can be best friends with somebody who had sex with my ex-boyfriend.

So, in honor of the Witches of WeHo and female friendships everywhere, here is a tried-and-true list of all the basic bitches you need in your life so you can form your own Witches of WeHo or SoHo or Topeka.

Next Level Basic GUIDE TO FRIENDS

THE FRENEMY

We all have them—the ones who shift back and forth between friend and enemy. This is someone who you hang out with and pretty much get along with, even though there are feelings of jealousy or competition simmering deep down, beneath your spray tan. You might not ask them to officiate your wedding or come over at 3:00 a.m. with some wine and Twizzlers, but life would be so boring without the drama that comes with the frenemy, am I right? Shout-out to Scheana Shay.

THE CHILDHOOD BFF

This is the closest thing you get to true flesh-and-blood family. There's nothing like the comfort of being around your childhood best friend, the one who loved you through all your weird phases and failed relationships and life changes. Plus, the inside jokes and references you have with the childhood BFF are like no other (and make sense to no one but you guys, which kind of makes you feel like you're in an exclusive, superfun cult).

THE TRAVEL BUDDY

It's already so hard to find people you travel well with. It sucks going overseas with someone only to find out that they love to plan every single second of the day while you like to wake up at noon and wing it, or that they only want to eat at McDonald's in whatever country you're in while you want to eat at random street vendors with no Big Mac in sight. Finding a BFF you travel well with who can also take off work *whenever*? Hard to find. It's like the Holy Grail. Find her.

THE SHOT TAKER

Because sometimes you just wanna get hammered, you know? Some people feel like doing shots past the age of, like, twenty-four is embarrassing or immature (whatevs), so we all need the friend who DGAF about arbitrary drinking rules and is always there for you when you want a shot, whether you're twenty-one or forty-one.

THE TOUGH LOVER

That one friend who will always tell it like it is, even if it's not what you want to hear. She isn't going to sugarcoat anything, and it might sting in the moment, but you know she's looking out for you, so it's all good. Katie Maloney is the ultimate tough lover—I know that whenever she opens her mouth to give advice, it's about to get real.

THE MOTHER

This is one of my faves. The friend who loves to just "handle shit." She loves to be in control, loves to make phone calls on your behalf, loves to organize. When you're with this one, you can just sit back and relax and trust that shit's getting taken care of. This is Kristen Doute for me. The girl takes care of shit.

THE GOSSIPER

I swear there have been actual scientific studies that show that "gossiping" bonds people. I mean, as long as it's not super mean-spirited, it's fine. It's fun! And we all need that friend who has *all* the gossip. They're true gems.

THE ZEN MISTRESS

Everyone needs one of these to keep us grounded and centered. They're always so mentally/emotionally stable, it's inspiring! Whatever they're putting in their green juices, I need some.

THE TALKER

I talk for a living. On *Vanderpump Rules*, on my podcast, in interviews. Most of the time when I'm not working, I kind of want to just sit back and shut up. So having a friend who *loves* to talk (extra points for a fast talker) is a key player in my book.

THE WTF FRIEND

Everyone has that one person they love and stick by, even when people are like, "How are they friends, WTF?!" It's the WTF friend, and this species is a ride-or-die. People are always shocked that I'm BFFs with my ex-boyfriends' girlfriends. But I strongly believe that your ex's girlfriend pool is one of the best places to find friends. Why? Because if your ex had good enough taste to choose you, then the next girlfriend or boyfriend *must* be just as cool. I always say Jax Taylor has the best taste in women because I found two of my best friends using this method: Rachael O'Brien (who came before me) and Brittany Cartwright (whom he is now engaged to marry). And did I mention I'm a bridesmaid? Despite what you may think, I am actually genuinely happy for Jax and Brit. I mean, Jax and I broke up eight years ago. So, good riddance . . . and best of luck to you, Brit!

The WTF friend relationship might shock people, but it also proves that you are actually a badass and you understand that true friendship means getting over your differences—and getting over yourself.

Next Level Basic TAKEAWAY

The female friendships in my life have been way more important than any of the romantic relationships I've been in. It might not seem like it at the time, since dating can be dramatic AF, but bonding with your girls (or guys) will get you through. You can be 100 percent yourself with your true friends, they're always there at 3:00 a.m. when you need them, and they're there to remind you where you come from, to help you through the tough times, and to do shots with you when no one else will. Friends are like chosen family, and that should be cherished.

CHAPTER 9

Get Yours

Guess what, y'all? It's the twenty-first century, which means that no woman should have to sit there sipping her drink as she waits for a guy to come and pick up her fucking handkerchief. I mean, I *also* love for men to make the first move because everyone wants to be chased a bit and feel like the chick in *The Notebook*, but there is no shame in being the one to make a move first. I just really believe that if you see something you want, you should act on it instead of being passive. Plus, I feel like women are just inherently more skillful at making the first move. Men often have a way of seeming douchey or cheesy when they try to pick someone up, but it's much more effortless for us. Sometimes it just takes a little work to get the confidence to actually do it.

Women have been conditioned to be the ones who *accept* something or *give something up* when it comes to sex and dating. We *accept* an invitation to a date, and if we're sexual, then we're *giving something up*. Why the eff is that? Why do we have to be passive? And it starts early! I went to an all-girls Catholic school and what they should have been teaching us instead of how to bake fucking blueberry muffins in home economics was teaching us about the DMV or how to do our taxes and plan financially for the future. Why do I need to make the perfect banana pancakes? I've never understood that. My generation (and all the generations before that) got taught that you have to wait for a guy to ask you out (I guess while you sit around making banana pancakes), or else you seem needy and desperate, instead of seeming like someone with confidence who knows exactly what she wants. That's changing, but I still see this old-school attitude at play way too often IRL. So maybe we should start a movement—tweet me with your #NLBGetYours stories so we can celebrate women getting out there and making a move, instead of sitting around being passive!

So Catholic school lessons aside, my parents raised me to be a strong person, and because of that I think I swung *too* far in the opposite direction at first. As a teen, I didn't want to be someone who would wait for a guy to ask me out, and I thought that demanding things would make me more powerful and not just a "girl" who had to sit around waiting for someone to come to me and tell me I was worthy. Now I think it should just be an even balance—you don't have to be a super aggressor, but you should also have the freedom and confidence to do what you want when you feel the impulse to do it. If you don't put yourself out there how are you going to accomplish anything, dating or otherwise? Believe it or not I can be bashful AF, but I also have no problem being the aggressor when it comes to dating. In fact, I made the first move with Jax, Patrick, *and* my current boyfriend, Beau.

Yes, it can be terrifying to make a move, and yeah, it *can* be embarrassing. In my early twenties, Kristen Doute had been trying to set me up with guys because I was young and single and working at Sur, so why not? She asked what my type was, and I answered, "I don't know—a hot dude?" (*Deep!*) She immediately said she had the perfect guy for me (I mean, there was only *one* qualification). She showed me Jax's Facebook, and I was like, "Perfect, sign me up." It took a while to get us at the same place at the same time, but finally one night I went out after work and saw him at the bar. Since he'd already messaged me on Facebook I decided to approach him and buy him a shot. I mean, what could possibly go wrong?

So I walk up, hand him a shot, and confidently say, "Hi, I'm Stassi, the chick you've been messaging on Facebook—do you want to do a shot?" And then he hard-core turned me down— *because he was on a date with another girl.* It was so humiliating that I just walked away (and did both shots, obvs). It was awful *but* it's not like I died or the world exploded. We ended up remeeting a year later in Vegas, and when we were reintroduced

I said, "Hi, you're the dude who turned down my shot." And we ended up dating. So getting humiliated gave me a pretty good second-time opening line, if you want to look at the bright side of the situation (and ignore the amount of time I wasted on a guy who was totally not right for me).

With Patrick, I had been a listener of his radio show for a while, and Katie Maloney kept telling me to reach out to him since we had similar cynical, dark, sarcastic senses of humor. So one morning I was supes hungover and was listening to his show, and he was talking about soul mates. I think the hangover made me extra bold (plus I had Katie and Tom encouraging me), so I publicly tweeted at him something like, "Listening to your show on soul mates, next time I'm in NY I'll pay you a visit." (*I know, I know.*) It was risky and kind of ridiculous, but again, the world didn't end, and I didn't drop dead of embarrassment. He followed me on Twitter right away and responded in a flirty way, and that initial tweet turned into a long-term (on-again, off-again) relationship.

And I didn't stop there. With Beau, *both* Kristen and Katie knew him and had been wanting to introduce me to him for two years. They always told me about him between my break-ups with Patrick, and since we broke up like every other month, they told me about him a lot. One day after Patrick and I had broken up for good, Kristen hosted a party for the Mayweather-Pacquiao boxing match, and she asked me to come because Beau was there. I was totes not in the mood to put on makeup and try to look pretty, but I forced myself to get glam(ish) and go to a party for a boxing match that I wanted to watch as much as I wanted to watch a documentary about the fundamental theorem of algebra. I hung out with my friends for a while and ignored Beau completely, but I guess I was bored of the boxing or I just got that impulse and I eventually got up, marched my ass up to Beau, and was like, "Hi, I'm Stassi," in a pretty hard-core aggressive tone. I also made the first move with him sexually, so there's that. I mean, I could have gotten rejected, and that would have sucked for like ten minutes, but it ended up working out— because I made a move.

I'm not saying it's always easy, or that it always works, but I am saying that it's *possible*. You just have to get your ass out there and march yourself over to someone (or tweet at them). I gravitate toward unapologetic women, so for the most part I think all of my friends are women who would make the first move or at least find no shame in that. Katie and Tom's love story makes me proud! I remember her sitting on my couch after they had been dating for a few months and she was scared to commit. We sat and talked about it until she finally admitted to me that Tom was it for her. So the next day, she asked him to lunch and said verbatim, "Do you want to be my boyfriend?" And he didn't run off or throw a drink in her face. He said, "Well, I don't know if I'll be any good at it . . . but yes." And now they're married. See—women making the move is a powerful-ass thing!

I've been the third wheel in Katie and Tom's relationship since day one. I lived on their couch for a while; I went to dinner with them. I was basically like their child. Before their wedding we joked that I should go on the honeymoon with them, and halfway into their honeymoon they called me and told me to come—to Bora Bora! I guess they thought Bora Bora was boring boring. So I got a ticket and it was the most intense travel I have ever experienced. I had to take planes, boats, golf carts, and canoes to get to this resort. It was *all* couples, and people were so confused by the dynamic between Katie, Tom, and me. But to us it was totally normal. I mean, I had my own bungalow with champagne and rose petals, so it's not like I was cuddling up with them at night or anything!

Right now, you are probably wanting guaranteed tactics that will help you approach people you're attracted to and never get rejected so you can honeymoon in Bora Bora like Katie and Tom (and me). But when it comes to 100 percent guaranteed tactics, I have No. Fucking. Idea. It's not about having a certain line or making the perfect move. You have to be in a place in your life where you don't care about maybe, possibly being embarrassed for five seconds. You have to be willing to say, "I would regret this if I didn't do it." I mean, why do you have to sit around and wait for dudes to come up to *you*? How stupid is that? When it comes to tactics, I just pretend I'm the most confident person ever. I play pretend, and it has worked out for me this far. And I *know* you can at least *pretend* to be confident AF. So next time you're out and you see someone you like, just fake it if you have to and walk up to them as if you're the love child of Beyoncé, Gisele Bündchen, and Scarlett Johansson. If it doesn't work, I swear you will live to try it on the next guy.

Instead of handing you some BS tips about how to make a move and never fail (because we *all* fail sometimes, and that's okay), there is a simple quiz on page 110 that will hopefully remind you that making a move is not nearly as terrifying as public speaking, skydiving, or being buried alive.

Next Level Basic TAKEAWAY

Like I said, it's messed up that women have been conditioned to be so passive when it comes to sex and dating. We're making changes and making the first move more than our moms and grandmothers did (unless your granny was a badass), but that sit-around-and-wait-for-the-guy-to-pick-up-the-handkerchief mentality is something we still have to fight. Each time I make the first move, it boosts my confidence and reminds me that walking up and talking to someone is NBD. I know I'm not invincible and that it's always possible that the guy might reject the shot I give him because *he's on a date,* but I also know that if that happens, I'll live. And you will too.

NEXT LEVEL BASIC QUIZ: MAKING THE FIRST MOVE

1. If you walk up to a guy in a bar and ask his name, the following will happen:

    A. You will literally die of embarrassment.

    B. You will melt like the Wicked Witch of the East, leaving only your shoes.

    C. The guy will tell you his name and you'll start talking.

2. The best way to get someone's attention is to:

    A. Sit back, keep your eyes down, and look terrified.

    B. Strut around like you're Jennifer Lawrence in a Dior ad and make eye contact with anyone you're interested in *because you can.*

    C. Stay home, watch movies, and avoid all dating apps and social events until your soul mate comes and knocks at your door holding out two tickets to Paris.

3. You're at the airport, your flight is delayed, and you see someone hot sitting at the lame airport bar. You should:

A. Buy some $15 trail mix and $8 water and go sit at your gate alone, thinking about the hot guy at the bar who you will never meet.

B. Stare at the hot person from outside the bar, fantasizing about them seeing you and leaving their drink to come talk to you because you are *that* amazing. (Which they never do, BTW.)

C. Get your ass to the bar, sit next to them, order a $25 martini, and ask where they're traveling.

D. Sit at the other end of the bar, order a crappy $18 glass of wine, and smile at them.

E. Either C or D.

4. **When approaching someone you think is hot it's always best to:**

A. Rehearse your "line" eight thousand times until you sound like a robot on crack.

B. Take a deep breath and remember that *they're just a fucking person.*

C. Freeze up, grab the hand of your nearest friend, and run out of the bar/club/restaurant like a psycho.

D. Let your inner voice that's saying *This is so lame, you're going to mortify yourself* win out over the other (better) inner voice that's saying *You've got this, go talk to them and be your confident, badass self.*

5. Making the first move via social media is:

A. NBD.

B. Something only a lunatic would do.

C. Okay if you have no shame and don't mind literally dying of embarrassment.

D. Only acceptable if you're Madonna, Idris Elba, or Beyoncé.

Answers

1. C

2. B

3. E

4. B

5. A

SECTION III

Hot AF

CHAPTER 10

Style Confessions

I went to Catholic school, and my very first confession as a kid was about fashion. (My clothes didn't match, and I guess I felt that was *a sin that I needed to repent for*!) I just cared deeply about what I wore to receive the sacrament, and I've cared deeply about what I've worn pretty much every day since. It's actually kind of exhausting.

When my parents got married and had me, we lived with my grandparents for a long time, and my grandmother (who is my style icon) would sew me dresses. I used to change like three times a day, so even as a toddler I wanted to wear as many outfits as I possibly could in one day. My grandmother is always dressed to the nines: matching jewels for every outfit, matching jackets

for every pair of pants, handbags for each outfit. It's so over-the-top, but in a classic way. She just loves a good chunky necklace, and she's always been glamorous, so from an early age I wanted to be like that—so I blame her for creating a monster.

Even with all my childhood and teen years spent obsessing over fashion, it still weirds me out that people look to me for style advice. I mean, every single day I pace around my apartment sweating my ass off, feeling like I am disgusting and that I have nothing to wear (I live in LA and don't have central AC). Then I go to my memory box of who I look up to as far as style, and I pray to the style god like, "Please bestow some creativity upon me so I can look decent today." So I need help too! And it's just surprising (and flattering) that other people would say things like *What would Stassi wear?* I mean, I'm already struggling enough as it is.

Some people believe that loving fashion is shallow and basic *in a bad way*, and those people obviously have no sense of humor and no friends. Stay away from them. Fashion is about self-expression and creativity and culture (and, yeah, sometimes it's about looking hot). In Catholic school I was always getting in trouble for my nail polish and my accessories, but it was the only way I could express myself. One regulated piece of jewelry isn't enough self-expression IMHO. What you wear can say so much about who you *are*, so why would you *not* care about fashion?

As a kid, I was always giving my friends fashion advice, whether they wanted it or not. I remember helping my friend Saint Alex (aka the breakup nanny) pick out a winter formal outfit in high school. Instead of going to the mall or a department store, I challenged her to let me take her to Goodwill with five bucks to put together her winter formal look. I found her this beautiful black strapless dress with these light-pink iridescent shoes, and later we made pink beaded straps for the dress to tie in with her shoes. I was so proud that she looked phenomenal *and* it was five bucks *and* I found it at Goodwill (she also had and has a perfect body, so that def added to the outfit). In college I decided to major in English because I loved writing and reading and thought that maybe one day I could just write about clothes (like right now). Then it took on a life of its own and I started writing fashion blogs. My style may not be for everyone—it might be a little too girly and a little too sparkly at times—but I noticed that people were calling me a "style maven" in articles and I was like, *Cool. That's weird . . . but cool.*

But my style wasn't (and isn't) always perfect. I mean, I went through a ton of embarrassing fashion phases that I am going to confess to you right now, but the thing is—figuring out who you aren't helps you figure out who you are, right? And it also helps you get closer to your unique look.

Embarrassing AF Fashion Phases That Helped Me Find My Look

SPICE GIRLS STAGE

As you now know, I was obsessed with the Spice Girls. I feel that it's important to state that this was during that Limited Too, late nineties, Y2K era. I wore overalls with smiley faces, peace signs, and yin-yangs on them, and there was a yellow patent-leather smiley-face backpack, and I begged for that *for months* for Christmas. That year I spent so much time staring at the gifts under the tree with a scowl on my face because my mom wrapped the backpack without a box, so it was *in the shape of the backpack*, so I knew what it was and I was like, *This is bullshit! Give me the yellow patent-leather smiley-face backpack!* Life was tough. This was also the phase of glitter, metallics, and silver eye shadow. I'm glad it's over.

HIGH FASHION

PREPPY STAGE

I maybe regret this one more than any other phase. I'm talking Doc Martens, but not like the hard-core Goth kind, like the preppy kind. They're not flattering on anyone, and here I am this

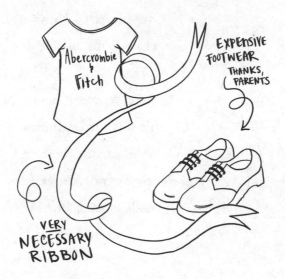

twelve-year-old girl with giant Doc Martens on my feet and Abercrombie T-shirts. That shit was so expensive; I feel bad for my parents. My hair was always in a ponytail . . . *with a ribbon.* I love a good ribbon now, when it's done right, in a high-fashion way, but a ribbon when you're twelve years old and wearing Abercrombie is just . . . *no.* I'm not going to blame myself too hard for this one. It's just what everyone was doing in New Orleans, so I followed along.

DEBRA MESSING STAGE

At the start of high school I decided I would stop being a follower. I was like, *I'm going to be* me! So I dyed my hair bright red because I loved Debra Messing in *Will & Grace.* I decided that I loved being girly and glam and that I was going to embrace that, no matter what. I wore fake flowers in my hair with my ugly Catholic school uniform. I would also change my nail color every day to express myself, and I mean, that is fucking commitment. Mind you this was the beginning of my awkward phase. These were not pretty times, no matter how great my nails looked. But I tried.

THE DREADED UNIFORM

WANNABE GOTH STAGE

I never truly committed to being Goth. I mean, you never saw me with black eyeliner running down my face. Each summer I would be home from school every day, looking in the mirror going, *Who am I?!* So I would reinvent myself through fashion. During this phase I was watching a lot of Eva Green and Angelina Jolie and Liv Tyler movies and I was like, *This is who I am! I'm not the redheaded girl or the blond girl, I am this dark person!* Angelina Jolie wore gray lipstick and I was like . . . that's cool! I'm doing that. And it's not like I was going to GothicPeople.com, I got that tip from a fashion magazine. Black hair and gray lipstick is really not an aesthetic for anyone

FREE
WINONA

SHADES TO HIDE MY SHADE

CAN YOU FEEL THE ANGST?

other than Angelina Jolie, but I tried. I also wore that "Free Winona" shirt constantly, and my dad would take me to LA on trips and I would wear that with some huge five-dollar cheap glasses and I felt like a (Goth) movie star. So freaking embarrassing.

PARIS HILTON STAGE

This is just as embarrassing as the preppy phase because Paris Hilton isn't really one to look up to style-wise, you know what I mean? This was the whole Paris Hilton–Nicole Richie–Lindsay Lohan era when they were BFFs. I dyed my hair blond again and got UGG boots and a white Balenciaga bag—but I couldn't afford a Balenciaga bag, so it was the one and only time I wore a fake one. I have strong opinions about wearing fake bags. I would rather wear a five-dollar vintage bag than wear anything fake. Knockoffs irk me. That was not hot, as Paris says.

All these phases happened in high school (I was really searching for who I was fashion-wise, I guess), and by the time I started college I had settled into my own look that wasn't based off a movie star's look or a yellow patent-leather backpack. I started tearing photos of looks

I liked out of magazines and making collages, and I still have all of my collages to this day. They're my prized possession. Now that I'm older and my body is changing it's even more important to have a look that works for me, because deciding on an outfit can be stressful. I'm twenty pounds heavier than I was in my early twenties and my ass is flatter than ever before, which seems weird, right? How do you gain weight *and* get a flatter ass? It's the miracle of aging. So when I do get stressed about what to wear I just try to think of what my grandmother would put on, and it helps. My grandmother is like fashion Xanax.

Besides my grandmother, I look to people like Olivia Palermo as style inspirations, but her body is the opposite of mine, so I can't wear everything she wears. I've learned to look for inspiration from women who have my body type so that I'm not setting myself up for failure. Enhancing what you have is more important than what's in style. Now I look at Chrissy Teigen and Kate Upton for inspiration—people who I feel like I have a connection to because of their body type. That's key—realize what works with your body and who you really are, and start from there. . . .

Next Level Basic STYLE TIPS

KNOW YOUR BODY

Knowing what looks good on you is the most important thing when it comes to finding your look. That said, I don't follow any "body type" rules and I definitely break the rules when it comes to wearing things that are meant for big boobs or pancake butts. Knowing your body means figuring out what you want to enhance and what you want to cover up, not figuring out whether you're a pear or an apple. Take some time to understand what makes you feel comfortable, and once you recognize that, you can start your style collage.

GET INSPIRED

Once you get your body type down you can look for inspiration in magazines or online* and make a collage of looks that inspire you. Whether you're using a glue stick and cardboard or Pinterest, store a bunch of photos that inspire you. Once you have enough, look

---

* Quick Word of Warning!
Remember that this can be dangerous because everything is photoshopped. I can easily spiral into a major Instagram depression and start having dark thoughts like, *Why does everyone have a twenty-inch waist, a giant butt, and big boobs? I don't understand!* We have to remind ourselves that what we see on social media is mostly altered. This is why I make it a huge point not to alter my photos too much anymore—unless it means putting a million filters on them because, let's be real, filters don't count. I use filters, but heavy airbrushing makes me depressed. I don't want someone to meet me in person and say, "You are so much prettier on Instagram." So while I advise you to look at magazines and Insta, you have to remember that nothing is real, so don't get down on yourself!

through them and you'll see a theme and a pattern emerge. Then you'll recognize your style and it'll be easier for you to shop. Say you look at your collages and there are like five one-shouldered Grecian flowy dresses—that's a sign to go find one! I am all about seeing how many versions of one article of clothing I can obtain in every color and every fabric. Sometimes if I can't find a piece in other colors or fabrics I'll bring it to my seamstress and ask her to make it. Or I'll search online for similar styles and colors so I can keep my "uniform" going. Finding something you like is totes important.

GET A UNIFORM

In a way, finding your personal style means having a uniform. We can't all just walk around every day in new and different outfits; we're not Kim Kardashian. So find a uniform you love and then tweak it. During the fall I love tight, skinny boots with a skirt and oversize sweater. I take that formula and find them in different fabrics and styles and colors, and I mix and match. I found what works and what makes me feel comfortable. During the summer you can't get me out of these amazing OneTeaspoon brand denim shorts. They're oversize, so they don't pinch your back fat and they fall just so, so they make you look like they're just swallowing you up and you're so tiny! Then I pair them with an airy button-down and kitten heel. This look isn't skanky because the heels are two to three inches. Then I tweak it with different purses and accessories, so I'm just shifting the uniform.

GET COMFY

If I'm not comfortable I want to maim someone. There is nothing I loathe more than a bandage dress. My nightmares are made out of bandage dresses. The idea of standing there and sucking in all day and all night terrifies me. Sucking in is the least fun thing I can think of. I would rather spend an entire month without ranch dressing.

So maybe fashion is basic, but is that a bad thing? I say embrace your love of kitten heels and rompers and to hell with the rest. No one is curing cancer by putting together outfits, but it's a way for us to just be ourselves and express who we are. I wish I could shake my twelve-year-old self and be like, "Girl, do you, because you're going to look back and be like this gray lipstick was so not me!" Fashion makes us feel good when we not only look good but have on something that we feel represents us as a person and says to the world *this is who I am*. Once you have your look, no one can take that from you. So get yours!

Next Level Basic TAKEAWAY

Some people might think that fashion and style are frivolous things that matters less than, say, winning a Nobel Peace Prize. But even Nobel winners need to pick out an outfit for the ceremony! Style is about showing the world who you are inside, and my style trajectory started way back in Catholic school, as a form of rebelling. Making mistakes is nothing to be ashamed of (my Goth and preppy phases helped me figure out what I *definitely don't* want to wear), and it's part of the process of becoming your own Next Level Basic best self. So get out there and try black lipstick or sparkly platforms and see if they reflect who you are inside. If not, move on to the next look until you land on your signature.

CHAPTER 11

Who Wore It Worst?

W e've all made some pretty embarrassing fashion mistakes, right? I bet even *Vogue* editor Anna Wintour went through an awkward punk phase or a wannabe hippie era, but the photographic evidence is just probably locked in a vault in Switzerland or something. As for the rest of us, our WTF looks from the past might pop up on social media when an old frenemy posts a photo of us from eighth grade wearing patchwork overalls and a fedora, and we just have to deal with it. But all that said—when it comes to fashion, are there truly any "mistakes"?

Obviously the fashion world can be judgy (you saw *The Devil Wears Prada*, right?), but as much as I love to judge, I also believe that fashion is about self-expression (emphasis on the *self*).

Whether you're punk or bohemian, favor classic pieces or preppy clothing or supertrendy Kardashian looks, yours is really the only opinion that matters. We've all had our moments of *I can't believe I wore that!* Or the classic *WTF was I thinking?!* But at the end of the day, you thought those pink tweed culottes and gold headband represented who you were at that time, right? So here's a deep philosophical question for you: *How can there truly be such a thing as a fashion faux pas when style is about self-expression and the only person's opinion that matters is yours?* I think about this way more than I should.

It can take years to evolve your style, and after many phases, I'd call my personal style "easy feminine elegance" (totes emphasis on the "easy"). I think I keep it pretty consistent, and the more ladylike I look the more I feel like prancing around. Heels with sparkle put me in the best mood. I mean, worn the right way shoes that basically look like they have rhinestone necklaces on them *can* be elegant. Maybe some would call that a faux pas because glitter and sparkle aren't "classic" or "timeless," but whatevs. I also believe that affordable clothes that are timeless are key. So I shop at Revolve or H&M or Zara a lot—mainly because I sweat so much and use so much self-tanner that my clothes get ruined by pit stains or self-tanner blotches, causing me to have to replace pieces all the time, which isn't cheap. Restyling what you already have and own is key. Because who can afford to buy new outfits every month?

I wish I could say that watching myself on *Vanderpump* for years has helped me realize my fashion mistakes, but honestly there really hasn't been a moment where I full-on cringed at what I was wearing. Even if I wasn't into a particular outfit later on, I still recognize that I loved that look at that time. I do love a good fashion evolution, but I admit that I also second-guess my outfits *all the time*. I do not have it down yet. Sometimes I will put something on and leave the house feeling great and then a few hours later I catch a glimpse of myself in a window reflection or at an appointment and think, "What the fuck am I doing sitting here in this outfit? I look like a freaking White Walker!" But you live and learn.

We all have different tastes, different bodies, and different ideas about what looks good and makes us feel amazing. I loathe those articles in magazines about "The Five Things Every Woman Needs in Her Closet" or "Six Items for Your Weekend Getaway." There are no rules, and we don't all need to be mindless Stepford Wives with the perfect white button-up, the perfect pair of dark-washed skinny jeans, black ballet flats, and a great red lipstick. Just, no. I mean, unless that's your thing. But why the eff does every woman need a crisp white button-down (although I do love a classic white button-down)? We shouldn't feel pressured to own one (unless you really love them). Every woman should make her own list of five things that make her life easier and fit her own style, but it definitely doesn't have to be based on what a magazine says.

All that said, this book is technically about me, so while I don't agree with set fashion rules, I *do* have opinions and I'm only human, and there are things that I personally believe should have *never* been in style or trending *ever*. I realize that making this list goes against everything I'm saying, but because this is my book and I'm expressing myself, I am going to reveal the trends that I feel should go away forever. But hey—if you love them, knock yourself out.

BIRKENSTOCKS AND CROCS

A lot of people will disagree about the Birkenstocks, since they're trendy again, but they're just not flattering *at all*. They do nothing for my legs or my body except make me look like Jesus. I never understood why I would voluntarily choose shoes that make me look *worse*. As for Crocs—this is pretty self-freaking-explanatory. I almost broke up with Katie as a friend because she told me she got Crocs with flames all over them—because she said it reminded her of the *Diners, Drive-Ins and Dives* chef Guy Fieri. I was like, "Katie, this friendship might not work anymore . . ." But then I took a step back with my Crocless feet and was like, "You do you, Katie! You wear those flaming Crocs—just not in front of me."

SHORTS/SKIRTS WITH UGGS

UGG boots serve a purpose when it's freaking freezing and you want your feet and ankles to stay warm. I mean, WTF else do you wear? But denim minis with UGGs? It defeats the whole purpose. I want to know who first decided that this trend was ever a good idea. There should be a research paper written about the person who was like, "You know what would be really cool, man? If we just put UGGs with, like, jean shorts." I'm so glad that's done, and I pray it never comes back.

JUICY SWEATS/TRACKSUITS

This trend wasn't as bad as Birkenstocks, or UGGs with jean skirts, but this look is lazy AF in a thirteen-year-old-girl way. It's great for preteens, but we can do much better than this as adults. It's like the world is our fashion oyster and we're just going to head over and get a neon-green velour Juicy suit? With UGGs? I mean, I'm all for easy (remember, easy feminine elegance), but this is just embarrassing. Tracksuits remind me of Scarlett Johansson and Ewan McGregor from that sci-fi movie *The Island*. I mean, are we in the dystopian future where we all have to where the same god-awful tracksuits? Kill me now. I originally got into tracksuits because I thought I was doing it in a chic way, but, like the Juicy trend, we have so many options—and we're just going to go for a tracksuit? I believe this look is only okay if you're at an actual track meet or if you're going on a six-plus hour flight and you dress it up with some cute accessories or shoes.

CROSS-BODY COACH BAGS

This one might be super specific to Y2K-era New Orleans, but this is my list and this trend deserves to be here (and only here). When I was living in New Orleans, girls (including me) wore these giant oversize North Face sweatshirts with cross-body Coach purses. Who decided that look was adorbs? My PhD theory about the cross-body Coach bag trend is that in New Orleans we're all a bunch of drinkers, so the Coach bags became a trend because they allowed you to double-fist your drinks. I appreciate the functionality, but they're still ugly AF.

CRAZY NAIL ART

Fashion shouldn't get in the way of you doing everyday things like making a phone call or opening your front door. If you have long tufts of fur on your nails (are you a werewolf?), or jewels hanging off, or LED lights glowing, how can you function? If I can hear your nails clicking on your phone, you need to do something different. Like get normal nails.

STEVE MADDEN SLINKY PLATFORM SLIDES

The shoe for us millennials during the late 1990s, and there is no scarier footwear (besides Crocs). To this day, I still get nightmares that this shoe is coming back in style. How did this shoe happen in the first place? It's clunky, ugly, and makes a weird slapping sound on the back of your foot when you walk. You know how this shoe could benefit humanity? If all murderers, rapists, and criminals had to wear them. That way, we could hear them coming from a mile away.

KARDASHIAN CHIC

I feel very passionately about this: Why am I seeing weird, unflattering, bizarre stuff on beautiful women? It's the freaking Kardashians. Much like cult leaders, I think they just decided that they can convince everyone to do anything they want so they're like, "Why don't we start wearing space suits and mini sunglasses and just see how many people copy us?" And the joke is on us. Part of me is like more power to them for performing this giant world experiment, because I'm pretty sure that's what they are doing (and they're also wearing Kanye's designs, so there's that). It's insane. Why else are people wearing tiny futuristic sunglasses (that serve no purpose) with a crop top, oversize space-looking cargo pants, and giant unflattering sneakers? I'm baffled. What's going to be next? Just like a giant plastic Versace bubble that they float around in? It's scary.

CLEAR PLASTIC CLOTHES

This trend is so unnecessary. It doesn't serve a purpose and only serves to make people sweat. Seriously, all I can think about when I see people in plastic outfits is, "That looks disgusting *and* you probably smell."

SUPERLONG SLEEVES

I've gotten offended when people have suggested I wear clothing with superlong sleeves. Do I have ugly hands or something? And what are you saying about my fingers? I'm talking those exaggerated long sleeves that flow past your hands like a wizard's gown. You can't wear a watch, bracelet, or ring. You can't even pick up a fork or a glass of pinot grigio without assistance. Why do this to yourself?

EXCESSIVE ATHLEISURE

Even the word "athleisure" is borderline offensive. Most of us aren't working out every single day, all day long—this is not a thing. Wearing workout clothes and sneakers isn't a "look." Wearing workout clothes and *heels* isn't even a "look" in my opinion. It's just laziness, or people just want to push the fashion envelope and see how far they can influence people into wearing the ugliest shit on the planet. And they're winning.

So again, if you love any of the looks on this list then that's . . . great. Hell, make your own Worst Trends in History list and put Stassi's easy feminine elegance at the top! Trends can be fun since you're adopting something new into your wardrobe that you're not used to and you're (sometimes) taking a "risk," but people who spend thousands of dollars on trendy pieces may need to recheck themselves. You have to be self-aware when it comes to trendy pieces. If that certain trend doesn't (track)suit you, then *don't do it*. Don't just blindly follow things for the sake of trying to be "in style," because having a great sense of style has nothing to do with trends; it's about finding a timeless look that is exactly who you are. But whatever you choose, do you, boo. If you feel like your best self in a clear plastic tracksuit with furry nail art, Crocs, and tiny space glasses . . . knock yourself out.

Next Level Basic TAKEAWAY

So remember when I asked the question: *How can there truly be such a thing as a fashion faux pas when style is about self-expression and the only person's opinion that matters is yours?* I hope by now you understand that although I personally believe that Crocs and Juicy sweats are morally offensive, that does not mean that you shouldn't own your fashion truth and rock them both together. The point though is to not embrace trends just because everyone else is—so the next time a mini skirt/UGG boot fad comes along you can be a little discerning, take a step back, and say, "Do I *really* want to wear a ski hat and a bikini, or am I putting it on just because I've seen five hundred Insta posts about it?" Be discerning when it comes to fashion trends, and you'll wind up with a lot less embarrassing photos to have to explain to your friends down the road.

CHAPTER 12

How to Look Hot on Social

There's a reason celebs always look amazing in their Instagram photos—even the ones "without makeup." Looking good on social is one of our most basic bitch desires as humans in the twenty-first century, and whether we like it or not, we live in a world where feedback on social media affects everything. We count the number of likes our selfies get on Instagram, we clock every retweet, and we smile when our best friends leave us a fire emoji on Insta. I mean, even my grandma in Louisiana is on Facebook, and she's over ninety years old. If she can embrace it, so can you.

I will say that I'm incredibly thankful that Instagram and Twitter didn't exist when I was a teenager. What a horrifying thought. It would have been a bunch of dark, broody posts about going to (and performing in) musical theater productions and me wearing Angelina Jolie's lipstick. You wouldn't have seen too many dudes with me at that time. Just moody AF posts and *Les Mis* memes. Or retweets of Paris Hilton and photos from *Moulin Rouge!* with hashtags like #Goals. I shudder and sweat even thinking about it. That doesn't mean I've never embarrassed myself on social as an adult. There have been times when I've been single and come home drunk and in an attempt to feel confident (and look hot) I would turn on weird music like Chris Botti and film myself doing stretches and (pseudo) ballet dancing in full makeup and hair, mouthing the words to depressing opera songs, thinking I looked amazing. And then in the morning I would wake up and be like, *Oh no . . .* #Embarrassing.

Today social affects everything—dating, jobs, friends. How would we even meet romantic interests now without Bumble or Facebook or Tinder? By bumping into them in a bookstore or starting a conversation at the post office? Please. Plus, being able to stalk someone a little when you're first dating them is crucial. You can make sure they don't seem like a murderer and you can also weed out dudes who have excessive gym selfies with hashtags like #Fit #GymDay #LaLaLand #WorkingOut #Gym #Headshots. I could go on.

We live in a time where branding is everything, so one thing can go wrong on social and everything comes crashing down on you, career-wise. Social media helps with my job, but it has also gotten me in trouble. It happened to me with my podcast sponsors (more on this later). Or what if you're applying for jobs and you have a public Insta with a bunch of skanky photos? Any boss can see that and judge, which sucks. But even with all the ups and downs of social media there is one universal truth: we all want to look hot AF. No one has ever taken a photo and said, "I hope I look ugly in it." We should just accept this fundamental human desire.

Where it becomes a problem (IMHO) is when it's nothing but a facade and you're abusing the Facetune app and your body is miraculously taller and skinnier than it is IRL. I love a good pretty filter, but when we make other people feel less than by putting out a fake AF version of ourselves, it's not cool. We're all morphing into each other with big lips and big butts and big boobs and a teeny tiny waist, like a cartoon. I say embrace what makes *you* unique and then find out how to be hot as *that* person instead of trying to look like what you think others want. Basically, be the hottest version of *yourself.*

We all *want* to look hot on social 24-7, but despite what the filters say, we're human and sometimes we are going to look not so hot. When I have psoriasis outbreaks or zits I sometimes make it a point to post photos without makeup, because it's *real.* It makes me feel better that other people comment like, "I can't believe you actually look like this sometimes—this makes me feel better about myself." Those comments inspire me to post more photos like that. I look at people like Bella and Gigi Hadid on social and it looks like their waists are sixteen inches and their asses and boobs are perfect, and I don't understand! I never see photos of them looking human, and it makes me feel like an ogre, which is so not cool. Looking hot on social means—yes—picking the best angles and using a filter here and there, but it doesn't mean looking so "perfect" that you set an unrealistic standard. And so, to help you look like the best version of yourself (on good days and bad) I present . . .

Next Level Basic Tips:
HOW TO LOOK HOT ON SOCIAL

FIND YOUR THEME

Is your thing photos of you out at clubs? Maybe photos of you staying in with your dogs? First, figure out the theme or themes you're into, and work with that. Maybe it's showcasing your style or your beach days or your food-truck obsession—narrowing down what you want to show (and project) will help make this a lot easier. For example, my thing is OOTD. I love documenting my outfits, and it makes me feel good to share photos of myself in a mirror (which makes you look longer and leaner) taken from an angle that works for me (I casually cross one leg over the other, tilt my head down a little, and I'm good). Finding a theme doesn't mean that every single photo needs to be you on a beach with an umbrella drink, but it does mean that finding *your* personal taste (whatever it might be) will help make it easier for you to post consistently—and feel confident doing it.

LEARN THE ART OF SMIZING

It gets exhausting to hold a big, giant smile. It looks beautiful, but it's tiring and sometimes you just want to look like a bratty bitch in your photos. Smizing (shout-out to Tyra Banks) is my fave way to look hot on social, but you have to practice. It's basically smiling without teeth and using your eyes to "smile." To smize, first imagine what makes you happiest, like Shake Shack or Chris Hemsworth, and let that emotion manifest itself from the eyes out. It's like you're thinking of something that makes the top of your head smile, while the bottom of your face is thinking of something gross like foie gras. My face twitched a lot when I first started practicing, but smizing will change your life, so keep at it. It's lazy hotness.

FIND YOUR FILTERS

Everyone I know has their fave filter (depending on my mood, I float between Aden, Valencia, and Gingham). Some people take this too far and they have a perfectly curated Insta account where every photo is the same color scheme and mood and it looks all uniform and shit, which bores me. I say use every filter there is, not just one. Don't just use Mayfair because some celeb uses it. Use what makes *you* feel good. You can also save a photo and then put a filter on top of the previous filter so you're not confined to just one (you're welcome if you didn't know that already).

FIND YOUR ANGLE AND YOUR LIGHT

Like smizing, you have to practice in order to find your perfect hot-on-social angle. It's embarrassing but . . . take hundreds of photos of yourself using different angles and see what looks good. It's a narcissistic-ass thing to do, but if you want to look your best you have to be willing to be a little bit of an asshole. Same with finding your light, which is something that actors and models spend hundreds of hours perfecting. It basically means discovering the most flattering place to be so that sunlight or overhead lights or the nearest lamp is making you look gorgeous. It takes some time to become a pro, so play around and you'll learn to find your light so that you don't look like a washed-out zombie.

EMBRACE YOUR FACE (OR YOUR ASS)

I am all for celebrities posting no-makeup selfies on social, but I have one major rule when it comes to doing it: if you're going to say you didn't use a filter and don't have on makeup, you best have no makeup on that face—and no filters or Photoshop either! I once posted a photo of myself during a psoriasis outbreak looking scarily like Gollum from *Lord of the Rings*. A friend (who shall remain nameless) posted a photo saying she was inspired by me to post a pic of herself with no makeup and no filters. I was flabbergasted when I saw it. I texted her saying, "You ho! You have false eyelashes on and you're practically in the dark!" She admitted that she used Photoshop to add fake eyelashes. That is so *not* hot. That said, I am all for whatever makes *you* feel good, whether that's lash extensions or microblading your brows. You don't have to do a makeup-free selfie if you don't want to, but if you do, especially in a sexy way—do not alter that photo. Let's be honest about what we're doing here, people.

Because I work hard to look good *on* camera, I try to sometimes embrace my face when it goes full Gollum IRL. I have also accepted my flass (flat ass, FYI). Having a big bubble butt is just not in the cards for me—I have a flass and it is what it is. Everyone—let's just embrace what we have (with a little Botox here and there for good measure if that makes you feel good)! Looking hot on social is not about being "perfect." It's about finding out what makes *you* feel next-level hot and going with that. We live in a world where we get confidence from comments or likes on social. I wish more people would encourage others to put themselves out there and be proud of whatever they have going on. I want to challenge everyone to "like" things or make kind comments (crazy, I know), and whatever you do, don't shame people. For better or worse, social media is a major way we gain (or lose) confidence, so let's embrace what we have and also be next-level *kind* about it—to ourselves and others.

Next Level Basic TAKEAWAY

We are all humans with egos and Instagram accounts, and therefore we all want to look good on social. That's nothing to be ashamed of! And while filters and lighting and the right pose can do a *lot* for a girl's ego, it's important not to believe everything you see online. So while you're taking steps to become a hot-ass basic bitch online, just remember that every celebrity is airbrushed and tweaked and professionally styled, and it takes practice to find your best angle, so have fun with it.

CHAPTER 13

Basic Beauty

The late, great comedian Joan Rivers has been an idol of mine since I was a kid. I love anyone who can bring humor to a topic that is often humorless, like fashion or beauty. I always loved that she could poke fun of herself and that she was brutally, hilariously honest about her nips and tucks and fillers and peels. I think that the ticket to being able to judge other people is being willing to judge yourself too, and when it comes to that, she was the queen. I mean, the point of fillers or Botox is to make us feel good about ourselves, but when you're getting all this plastic surgery and you're pretending that you just naturally look like that, you're just making people feel bad about themselves. Following Joan's MO, I've always been honest about my chin implant, my breast reduction/lift, and my love of a good spray tan. You think I'm naturally this bronzed? Please.

I am all for whatever makes you feel good, but at the same time it seems like everyone is suddenly walking around like a cartoon character. Human beings are not birthed this way! Everyone suddenly has the same body, yet no one is admitting to getting surgery. No one is ashamed of coloring their hair, so let's stop being dishonest skanks and fess up so people aren't looking at you thinking, *Why didn't I come out of the womb looking like that! WTF is wrong with me?!* That's just not cool. The truth is that everyone in Hollywood has had a little (or a lot) of work done, making everyone sitting at home watching them wish they could look that "perfect." So just know that there is nothing "wrong" with you—you just don't have the same doctors as them!

I'm all for some alterations here and there, but my idea of going "too far" is if I start to not look like myself. To each their own, and if you *want* to look like the Catwoman lady then go ahead, but I think it's about enhancing what you've got or fixing something you're insecure about, instead of trying to become a replica of some fitness model (who is lying about her hundreds of Brazilian butt lifts anyway—more likely she got butt injections).

My first memory of altering my appearance in the name of beauty was when my mom highlighted my hair when I was nine. Yep, nine. Just remember—I'm from the South. I told my mom I wanted a perm for my birthday and then changed my mind and decided I wanted to be blonder, and she said, "Great!" I

thought I was such a baller being a nine-year-old with highlights. The next beauty experiment was self-tanner, but this was right when self-tanner came out. I took a bunch of mini test tubes of Clinique free samples and slathered them on, and I ended up looking like a weirdly colored alien from some beach planet. This was legit a tester situation, and my teenage skin proved that this stuff did not look legit.

After that disaster came the chin implant my parents gave me as a high school graduation gift. If you're questioning their parenting skills, whatevs. They trusted my judgment, and I was desperate for a bigger chin and more defined jawline. Maybe they were sick of seeing me stick my chin out in photos, but whatever the reason, they said okay and the appointment was made. My mom was out of town and my dad was working the day of my appointment, so one of my best friends (shout-out to Sheena Mannina) took me to the surgery center and came back to my house and spent four days with me, feeding me Godiva shakes all day long. That's a recipe for #Obesity. My face swelled up from the surgery (and maybe the shakes) but it ended up being freaking awesome. It's one of the best things I ever did and to this day makes me feel better about myself.

The chin came first, but I had fantasized about a boob reduction and lift since I was twelve years old because I could literally nest a family of rats underneath my boobs they were so big and saggy, even at that age. Let me tell you, it is constantly uncomfortable to feel a heavy boob hanging like a pancake on your

stomach. When I finally met with a surgeon I told them that I didn't care about the scars—just butcher me up. It was the other best decision I've ever made because my nipples are now like seven inches higher!

I've also tried lip fillers and Botox, but I always make it a point not to get Botox when I'm filming because I hate it when people are having an emotion and you can't tell. I vowed to never get it while we're shooting *Vanderpump* so that people know when I'm mad at them. I loved getting my lips done even though it was one of the most painful things I've ever experienced. My boyfriend won't let me do it again because he thinks it makes me look like a baboon and he says I look perfect the way I am, so now I'm just stuck overlining my lips, but c'est la vie.

On the show, we all have our mini beauty disasters every now and then. With me, there have been so many scenes where I can see my hair extensions. IT'S SO EMBARRASSING. The damn tracks are so hard to cover up! I also have spray-tan issues, I'm *always* blotchy, and my armpits are always seventy shades lighter than the rest of my body. But the WORST BEAUTY DISASTER EVER. THE MOTHER OF ALL MOTHER BEAUTY DISASTERS? It was in season four, when I came back to the show after being away and I had to go meet with Lisa and film with her at Sur. I wore a kelly-green dress. Because I knew how important this scene was (it definitely wasn't going to end up on the cutting room floor), I decided to get my makeup and hair done professionally and called up this hair and makeup stylist I

had just met. When I showed up to his apartment he was so high and the whole place smelled like weed; I could hardly breathe. He quickly did my face, and when I looked in the mirror, it looked like I had zero makeup on except for *glitter* on my eyes. That was fail number one.

Then when he went to do my hair, in his state of highness, he realized he had accidentally let out the dog. No joke, my hair was damp, he freaked out, sprayed my damp hair with hairspray, told me it was a "beachy vibe," and left to go roam the streets and look for the dog.

As a dog lover I understood his urgency, but the bro shouldn't have gotten so high that the dog escaped. I did not look beachy, I looked like someone who had just stuck her finger in a light socket. I ran to my car and started crying (at the time I was actually living out of my car since I had just broken up with Patrick and hadn't yet temporarily shacked up with Kristen Doute). I drove to the Rite Aid on Sunset and Fairfax and started frantically putting on my makeup using the mirrors in the cosmetics section (I paid for the makeup FYI). My friend Rachael O'Brien met me there and fixed my "beachy" hair. To this day, I can't watch clips of that *Vanderpump* scene with Lisa. It gives me mad PTSD.

So as many of you probably understand, beauty can be extremely stressful and a lot of freaking work! So I am going to share some basic beauty tips with you now, even though (as you'll see) I am no expert or guru—I just know what works for me.

Next Level Basic Tips: BEAUTY BASICS*

GET TAN

If you have pale skin like me, try to look tan because when you look tan, you look more toned. That's straight-up science, my friends. I spray-tan *a lot.* Like a lot a lot. I feel better when I'm tan, and when I'm pale I feel like a pile of mush. So if you also feel like a pile of mush and need a confidence booster, get yourself a spray tan and thank me later. For big events the whole cast will go to Brit and Jax's and a pro comes over to spray us all down. In my everyday normal life, I go to cheap tanning places and the results are not that great because when I watch the show my armpits are white and I look dirty. I'm actually pretty lazy about it—so maybe don't follow my advice when it comes to tanning. Be better.

LUBE UP (YOUR FACE)

I had it rough in high school with full-on acne that nothing would clear up. I finally tried Accutane, which I don't even think is legal anymore. It was crazy—my skin peeled off like a lizard—but it worked! For a while. When I moved to LA the acne came back, so I went to get a facial and the woman asked me if I had tried using oil to wash my face. WTF? Why would I make my face *more* oily? But I tried only using a makeup remover wipe

---

* And I mean *basics.*

and then oils to wash my face, and it totally worked. If I would have known you don't need all these harsh chemicals it would have saved me a lot of stress in high school. I also have bad psoriasis breakouts, which are impossible to cover up. Vitamins have been the only thing that's worked. I take magnesium, D3+K2 (whatever that is), and CoEnzymated B-Healthy (whatever that is too). This concoction cleared up my psoriasis within a few months, so I full-on recommend this. But then again, everyone's skin is different, so find out what works for you. And please don't get mad if you slather oil on your face and then break out the next day. I'm just a girl, washing her face in a way that works for her. I am not a dermatologist. Finally, I moisturize with La Mer. It's expensive AF but . . .YOLO.

DIET AND EXERCISE (YAWN)

This is my least favorite subject. Is there anything more boring than someone talking about their diet or their SoulCycle class? I go through phases where I work out really hard, but they only happen about every two years and they last about two weeks. I've learned that I cannot work out alone. I need a partner to motivate me and go with me. This will sound awful, but when I want to lose weight I just eat one meal a day and delete all carbs. I'll have a "healthy" salad but cover it in tons of ranch and hot sauce, so I am not here to give health advice. I mean, sometimes I go through phases where I drink beer for lunch, and Bytox hangover patches count as a food group IMO (you stick them on your skin and they have vitamins and nutrients that seep in and help you get over the hangover). So the lesson here is: Don't do as I do.

SWEAT IT OUT

Besides eating lettuce and ranch dressing, I go to this place called Shape House, where they strip you down and make you sweat out every ounce of water in your body so you feel skinny AF, even though you want to faint. You wear a long-sleeved shirt and pants and they wrap you up like a human burrito in a hot foil wrap, and it's like running ten miles. You sit there and sweat for an hour and it's miserable. But I'm lazy and don't like working out, so I'm willing to try things. When you unwrap the tinfoil burrito the sweat pours into a crate like a tsunami—it's disgusting, and I love it.

FREEZE YOUR ASS OFF

So being a lazy AF person who would rather undergo torture than step on an elliptical machine, I've also tried cryotherapy (aka "cold therapy"), where you get into a chamber that's set at freezing temperatures—kind of like submerging yourself in a giant ice pack. It's supposed to be rejuvenating and healing, but it is about as pleasant as the sweatbox, and it's scary because you can't see anything in the room. It would be a horrible way to die, but it works for me, so I'll take the risk.

EXTENSION BASICS

I've been getting extensions for six years, and it's a love-hate relationship. They make my hair fuller and I can change the length on a whim, but it's a time-consuming pain (*and* it's expensive). But sometimes you have to suffer for beauty.

LASH QUEEN

I've never done lash extensions because I'm too rough on my face, so they'd probably just fall off, but a tint-and-curl service is phenomenal. It's like a perm for your lashes that makes them darker and curls them up. I did a press tour in Australia and a makeup artist recommended it, and since all the girls there were blond and tan and had incredible lashes, I was in. In the United States everyone looks like a Kardashian, but in Australia everyone looks like Kate Bosworth in *Blue Crush*. A lash tint and curl can be like a mini miracle, so I highly recommend it. I am much more of an authority on lash tints than I am on diets, so you can trust me on this one.

BONUS: MAKEUP BAG BASICS

LA MER MOISTURIZER: Expensive AF but legit the best moisturizer out there. I cringe every time I have to pull out my credit card to purchase it, but this shit is the most heavenly stuff ever.

GREEN PRIMER: This helps neutralize red skin, so, people with rosacea: LISTEN UP. If you don't already know about green primer . . . YOU. ARE. WELCOME. I use Make Up For Ever redness correcting primer (the green tube).

AIRBRUSH CAN FOUNDATION (WITH SPONGE): I could put this on in the morning, sweat all day long, go swimming in the ocean, cry for three hours straight, and this stuff would *still* stay on. I swear by it. Sephora Perfection Mist Airbrush Foundation or Dior Air-flash Spray Foundation work for me, and I spray them onto a damp sponge.

BRONZER FOR CONTOURING: I could write a serious love letter to bronzer. I'm not married to a certain brand or color. I love to collect and rotate all different kinds. Right now I use BECCA's Bronzed Bondi and Kevyn Aucoin's Siena.

HIGHLIGHTER: I learned how to highlight from an article I read about Meghan Markle, and this is my favorite part of doing my makeup. Highlighting gives me the same satisfaction as eating a pizza, no joke. I use RMS Beauty Champagne Rosé Luminizer if I'm filming or if I really want to look dewy. On a normal day, I'll use Kevyn Aucoin's Candlelight highlighter because it's a little more subtle.

BROW PENCIL: Just totally necessary. Brows frame the face. I use an Anastasia brow pencil to shape and comb my brows. Do not neglect your brows, people. They need serious attention.

CREAM SHADOW: Just a good light brown semimetallic cream shadow that will melt into the skin and look totally natural. For eyes that are quick and easy, I'll dab some cream eye shadow for depth by RMS Beauty and then lots of mascara (Roller Lash by Benefit). For nighttime eyes, I just smoke it out as much as possible with whatever eye shadows I have lying around. I don't typically use a lot of black eyeliner or eye shadow, as it can be harsh with my coloring. And I am absolutely useless when it comes to a cat eye (I'm too shaky for liquid eyeliner), so I tend to stick with easy blending.

EYELINER: I put some eyeliner on the waterline of my top lid to make my lashes look fuller. I rotate different brands and am currently loving the one by Charlotte Tilbury.

MASCARA: I swear by Benefit's Roller Lash mascara.

LIP LINER: I also can't live without Edward Bess lip liner in Natural. My worst fear is that one day I'll be confined somewhere without it.

CHAPSTICK: I have *hard-core* dry lips. So I put ChapStick over my lip liner. One of my best friends (Kristina Kelly, you've seen her on *Vanderpump Rules*) started an all-natural skin-care line called Heartspring. All her stuff is *handmade*. So because all the ingredients are all-natural, I'll put that one first and then layer Burt's Bees tinted lip balm in Red Dahlia, because I love the color.

Nothing is worse than when you get makeup done and it looks amazing but it's heavy and uncomfortable. There is no way to feel beautiful when you have a pound of concealer under your eyes. If you don't like to cake it on, don't! And if you like to be au naturel with zero makeup, GOOD FOR YOU. Just don't judge the rest of us because if blue lipstick makes someone feel like a Next Level Basic bitch, then that's beautiful. And not being ashamed of your beauty routine, whatever it may be? That's Next Level Basic. Having a beauty routine that *makes you feel good* isn't superficial; it's self-care. Some people like to meditate, and others like to take a time-out to get their lashes curled or apply some lip liner. Whatever makes you feel good, I say go for it.

Next Level Basic TAKEAWAY

The moral of the story is to do what makes *you* feel good, so whether that means a chin implant or going au naturel and letting yourself age gracefully (in which case, good for you!), there is no wrong answer. Unless you're doing something not because you want to do it but because society is telling you to do it. It has taken years to figure out what works for me (if you would have told me as a teen that I'd put oil on my face every night I would have thought you were psychotic), so whether you're the natural type or a Botox queen, own your basic beauty routine so you can look *and feel* like a badass.

HOW TO START YOUR OWN BASIC BITCH NATIONAL HOLIDAY

As I've said, I am no expert on life, but when it comes to #OOTDs I basically have a PhD. I believe that style is artistic and that expressing yourself with your outfit directly affects your inner self-confidence. When you have a great outfit on, your day is that much better, and in my opinion, you should honor that feeling with an #OOTD. I love it so much I even turned it into a national freaking holiday, like National Doughnut Day or National Sibling Day. Some people might think it's vapid, but with National #OOTD Day (June 30, FYI), the mission is about embracing your individuality and your unique style, and cultivating the most important quality a Next Level Basic bitch can have: confidence.

I've been posting an outfit of the day on Instagram and Snapchat for years, and I try my best not to bombard people with photos of me in a mirror wearing clothes. I mean, it's once a day and it's an Insta story or a snap, so they don't last that long! When I first started posting it kind of became a thing, and the creators of the style blog *Who What Wear* reached out to me and asked me to write an article about over-the-knee boots, and I almost died of happiness. My friends made fun of me for my #OOTD obsession, and then suddenly people were actually interested. Booya! In your face, friends.

I mastered the art of making people think I'm hotter than I am *and* I started a national movement.

You might say I'm superficial, but look what happened. Don't be shy about posting your own #OOTDs. Maybe no one will see it but you and your mom, but who cares? You don't do it to win a Pulitzer, you do it *because it's fun.* Why not post your outfits so the world can see, if that makes you feel good? If you see that your friends watched it or the dude you're dating watched it, you're like, *YES! I was looking good and now everyone knows.* And plus, *if you wear a cute outfit and you don't post a photo of it—did it ever really happen?* Let that one marinate for a minute.

In the early days of my #OOTD obsession, I had no idea what kind of lighting to use or what angle looked best. I basically looked repulsive, so I took fifty or more photos to figure it out and get it right, much like a PhD student perfecting a thesis. After taking millions of photos you learn your angle. The angle reigns supreme when it comes to mastering this skill. You want this to be a quick, easy thing, not a five-hour-a-day ordeal that makes you miss work and fall into a depression. Once you get it down, right before you leave the house you can be like, "Oh, I should snap this and I don't care if people make fun of me because it only takes me three seconds." Efficiency (and the right angle) is key.

So say instead of #OOTD your personal obsession is chili cheese fries, or long naps, or pedicures—you should start a national holiday promoting and celebrating your personal obsession (someone def should create National Nap Day, BTW).

Creating National #OOTD Day is probably the most extra thing I have ever done, so here's what you can do to *change the world* (or just your Insta feed) and create your own freaking holiday too.

Next Level Basic Tips:
HOW TO START YOUR OWN HOLIDAY

START GOOGLING

First of all, I have to give credit where credit is due and thank my boyfriend, Beau, for coming up with the idea of creating National #OOTD Day and pushing me to make it happen. When we first decided to try to make National #OOTD Day a thing, I had no clue where to begin, so I googled "How do you start a national holiday?" The first links were all about passing legislation and making it all official with lawyers and contracts. #OOTD didn't need to be a government-issued holiday that's in the calendars you buy at Barnes & Noble. It didn't need to be on the level of Christmas or Presidents' Day (yet). I just wanted it to be on the level of Instagram. Eventually I found the organization in charge of all the social-media holidays (Doughnut Day, Hot Dog Day)—and it's called National Day Calendar. So that's where you start.

BE PERSISTENT (OR HAVE A PUBLICIST)

I filled out the submission form on their site and then . . . never heard back. I checked in—twice—and nothing. Finally, my publicist reached out to them and we heard back (if you don't have a publicist I would just ask a friend to pose as your publicist because it's not like they check credentials). So be persistent and don't give up—a *national holiday* is at stake.

FIND A MISSION

The National Day Calendar organization said I needed a "mission"—a real reason for starting this holiday. It seems like a weird ask, because what's the mission of National Coloring Book Day or National Kiss a Ginger Day? Anyway, once I started thinking about it, I thought it could be about more than sharing a selfie of an outfit. It could be a movement to help boost people's confidence and celebrate each person's unique style, encouraging people to put themselves out there and be proud of it! *YES!* Let's have confidence and celebrate our individual style. Once I had a mission I became obsessed because it became philanthropic or whatever. It was getting Next Level Basic.

MAKE A SITE

The organization said I needed a website explaining the mission, so I hired someone to make the site and we got the social handles for the holiday. We submitted everything, proving we had followed all of their very official rules, and then . . . I was accepted! Then the shitty part came. . . .

PAY UP

Did you know that National Cookie Day or National Bean Day do not come cheap? I found out that the cheapest holiday you can buy is $17,000. And it goes up to $350,000 (you get more promotion or whatever)! Right now you might be asking whether I am out of my mind to write a $17,000 check for a holiday, and the answer is . . . maybe? But, whatever, and you're welcome! Now we have National #OOTD Day.

At the end of the process I drank my sorrows away because I had just spent $17,000 on something that wasn't even tangible. But then I received my proclamation stating that I owned a national freaking holiday, and I threw a giant party on June 30, which is now officially National #OOTD Day. Seeing how many people were responding to the holiday on social and sharing their photos was a major moment for me. #Blessed.

So if there's something you're truly passionate about (and you have between $17,000 and $350,000—plus money to spend on a website designer and publicist!) get out there and make a holiday out of it. If not, just do your thing, save some money, and celebrate it with your friends every year as if it *were* Christmas or Presidents' Day. All you *really* need is a hashtag.

CHAPTER 14

What's in My Bag (Uncensored)

All basic bitches love *Us Weekly*'s "What's in My Bag?" feature, where celebs explain why they have stevia packets or cake-batter-flavored lip gloss or a key chain from Idaho in their designer clutch. In fact, I have actually been one of the "What's in My Bag" celebs, and so the world found out that at one time I carried a crystal, a fringe key chain, and a biography of the actress Lana Turner in my bag. Revealing the contents of my bag may not have ended world hunger, but maybe it helped people zone out and relax for a few minutes, so I consider that a public service.

Us Weekly is right about one thing: purses are a window into your soul, and you can find out everything you need to know about someone, not by looking deep into their eyes but by peer-ing deep into their oversize tote or tiny clutch. The type of bag I carry depends on my outfit, the time of day it is, and how I'm feeling. The only time I'm doing an oversize bag is if I'm going to the airport. Oversize bags are worn by people who humblebrag about how "busy" they are all the time—you don't *really* need that much stuff to go to the cleaners and walk your dog, do you? My mom believes that the bigger the bag the smaller your body looks, and I kind of understand her logic, but no. No way in hell would I carry a giant bag around. I'm too lazy. I don't like mini bags either because—what's the point? If it can't fit my iPhone then WTF? I'm a medium-size-shoulder-bag girl, and the bag has to have a strap because where am I going to put my cocktail? If you have a glass of wine in one hand and a bag in the other, how are you supposed to Instagram story the party you're at?

If I were to do an uncensored, up-to-date "What's in My Bag?," you would find:

My wallet (obviously)

My iPhone (double obviously)

Lip liner and ChapStick

A hangover patch (just in case)

A mini notebook and pen (I don't understand people who take notes using their iPhone)

A travel-size Poo-Pourri (This stuff is genius—it's a little spritz bottle that you spray into the toilet bowl before you go that makes it seem like you poop roses.)

A compact with pressed powder

Hot sauce (A friend gave me mini sriracha packs for my birthday and it was literally the most thoughtful gift I've ever received.)

A mini bottle of vodka (For the times someone suggests lunch at places that just serve coffee—rude!)

When I'm single and going on dates I'll also skank it up a little and add:

Spare underwear (I know.)

A mini toothbrush

Extra contacts and drops

Sunglasses (In case you have to do the walk of shame, these are a *must*.)

And when I travel I might throw in:

Mini podcast recorder

iPad or laptop

A silk eye mask

Extra hot sauce

Mini lavender oil (I am prone to anxiety attacks, so this calms me down.)

Hand sanitizer

Xanax (or Tylenol PM)

A charger

Band-Aids (In case my shoes hurt.)

Now, since our bags are the window to our soul, there are certain items you'll find in every basic bitch's bag, whether it's a tiny clutch or a gigantic tote.

The Basic Bitch's Bag

A SOULCYCLE PASS that never gets used.

A CAN OF ROSÉ: She may even have her own travel straw.

CRYSTALS: Every basic bitch is all into crystals, so you know there's a rose quartz to bring them love and find a boyfriend, or a tourmaline for protection.

HAIR TIES: This is when basic bitches become *heroes*. It's the worst when you realize you don't have a hair tie and you're out somewhere and really need one, but there is that one girl who is there to give away a hair tie and save the day.

BODY SPRAY: I've never really understood this, but lots of girls carry this shit around. Especially the Victoria's Secret body spray. Like, how often do we need to be spraying our bodies throughout the day? Same goes for rollerball perfume. Hopefully you don't smell *that* bad.

GUM: Necessary.

NARS BLUSH IN ORGASM: It feels like legit every chick uses this blush. I get it; it's a universally flattering color. And okay, fine—I have it!

ADVIL/MIDOL/EXCEDRIN: Headaches, cramps, and hangovers plague the basic bitch.

A SEPHORA VIB CARD: Admit it. We've all got them. I'm VIB Rouge level, FYI, which is like being part of the royal family of beauty-chain stores.

SUNGLASSES: Which are referred to as "sunnies."

A SENTIMENTAL KEY CHAIN: Maybe it has the date you met your boyfriend engraved on it in gold, or maybe it has the name of your Chihuahua or whatever.

LUMEE PHONE CASE: I get it—we all want to look good in our selfies. You won't find a true basic bitch who doesn't own this phone case with built-in light. And if they aren't using it now, at *some* point in their lives, they had or will have one.

A LIP COLOR FROM A CELEBRITY'S LIP KIT: Most likely Kylie Jenner's.

There you have it. Maybe you have one or more of these things in your humongous tote, and if so, good for you. Especially if you have that hair tie—you're a real Next Level Basic bitch and I salute you.

Next Level Basic TAKEAWAY

A woman's bag is a window into her soul, which means my soul needs hangover patches and lip liner. Post a pic with a list of the funniest (and most basic) things you keep in *your* bag with the hashtag #NLBWhatsInMyBag so we can celebrate our basic bitch selves!

Eat, Drink, and Be Enlightened AF

CHAPTER 15

Cocktail Hour(s)

Most basic bitches love their cocktail hour. Whether it's brunch Bloodies, lunch pinot grigio, midday margaritas, happy-hour sangria, dinnertime wine, or late-night *whatever sounds good and is around* drinks, what and when you drink can become like a sacred ritual. The thing is, you can't just drink all day and night, get sloppy, and puke all over the Lyft at 2:00 a.m. That's not what this is about. Being Next Level Basic when it comes to drinking is about knowing your limits so you don't wind up twerking on top of a table (but if you do, YOLO). Over the years, I've perfected the art of the twenty-four-hour cocktail hour. Some people win Oscars or save orphans (or in Angelina Jolie's case, both), but I can get my drink on 24-7 and still wake up early(ish) for work. It's a life skill and a major accomplishment, IMHO.

If you watch *Vanderpump*, you might think everyone on reality shows is just wasted all the time, which isn't 100 percent true. It's maybe 95 percent true. I wasn't a lush as a teenager because I was too busy learning lines for musical theater. I didn't really go to parties or care about getting wasted, and maybe that's because my parents let me drink from a pretty young age, European-style. They always treated me like an adult and allowed me the occasional glass of wine or Kir Royale if we were in a hotel lounge and they were having drinks, so I wouldn't feel left out. It made drinking less of a mystery, so maybe that's why I never got wasted in high school. Until junior prom.

I went to the dance with my gay best friend, Jesse, who I met through musical theater. He had the brilliant idea to wear something fun like a tie-dyed tux, and I was all in. I found a beautiful red dress, and my aunt let me borrow these insane velvet feathered Prada shoes. When Jesse showed up in his tie-dyed suit we felt like seventeen-year-old ballers. My parents got a bunch of us a limo so we could go out on Bourbon Street after the dance, and looking back, I can't believe my parents let me get a chin implant, dye my hair, and ride around New Orleans in a limo as a teenager, but it's the New Orleans Way, so don't judge. When we finally got to the dance the nuns wouldn't let us in because they thought Jesse and I were dressed too un-Catholic, I guess. Eventually we persuaded them, but I was pissed! Nuns can be totes rude.

So after the formal we took the limo to Bourbon, and our sweet, patient driver had only one request: please do not puke in the limo. We went to the gay part of Bourbon, and in New Orleans you can get inside a bar at eighteen (plus we all had fake IDs), so we found ourselves in a bar with naked men dancing everywhere, which was much better than the Catholic school dance. I think I took every shot under the sun, because I didn't understand important rules like sticking to one type of alcohol (or not doing a million shots). It was my first time getting obliterated, and when we got back into that sweet limo driver's car I broke his one single rule and projectile puked all over the place, which was *super* basic, but *not* in a Next Level Basic way. Since then, I've learned my limits, and I have never puked in a limo again. So . . . sorry to that very patient driver who put up with my puking.

I joke all the time that I have chosen careers based on whether I'm allowed to drink on the job: I worked at Sur (drank on the job), I've been on reality shows (drank on the job), I have a podcast (drank on the job), I've modeled (drank on the job), and now I've written a book (definitely drank on the job, but that's what all good writers do! See: Hemingway). My résumé could include the types of drinks I pair with each job. I mean, isn't that why everyone moves to Los Angeles? To drink on the job? During our *Vanderpump* interview sessions, I either always bring white wine or beer and drink it out of a 7-Eleven Big Gulp cup—because interviews are *brutal*. Having to talk about things that happened six months ago? Especially if it's something emotional? The Big Gulp helps.

On the show, the "Crymax" is the drink we all would sneak and drink at Sur throughout our shift. The story is that me, Kristen Doute, and Katie Maloney would get to Sur and make this drink all night long. We would get away with it, because everyone just assumed we were drinking soda water and juice. Tom Schwartz named it the Crymax because 95 percent of the time, one of us ended up in the fetal position crying over our boyfriends. You could find us drunk and crying in the kitchen with the staff just staring at us like we were sad, drunk monsters, or in the parking lot out back by the dumpsters, or locked in the bathroom as the manager threatened to fire us. This drink was always the first sign that the night was going to end up with drama. I'd be crying over some girl Jax was texting with, Kristen would end up terrorizing Tom Sandoval all night long, and Katie would have her fits over Schwartz. And that was a standard Tuesday.

If you'd like to make your own Crymax,

here's what you need to do:

Fill a tall water glass with ice.

Fill the glass ¾ full with white wine.

Top off the final ¼ with club soda.

Add a spoonful of strawberry puree.

So we might drink on *Vanderpump*, but ever since my Bourbon Street limo incident I've worked hard to become a next-level drinker, which means no puking, no stumbling around, no losing control (well, not totally). When I hit my limit I just get mean and tired, which isn't fun for anybody. I like a few day cocktails and some at dinner and maybe a little afterward, but it's rare that I get fully *wasted*. So while I'm not an authority on life, I could teach a course called 24-7 Drinking Without Losing Your Shit.

WHAT YOU SHOULD DRINK

HOUR	BEVERAGE	
9:00 A.M. BRIGHT & EARLY		← BE SMART!
10:00 A.M. ACCEPTABLE TO NOW DRINK		
BRUNCH! 11:00 A.M.–1:00 P.M.		← THE MOST CHOICES
HAPPY HOUR 5:00 P.M.–7:00 P.M.		
DINNER 8:00 P.M.		← KNOW YOURSELF!
BED 11:00 P.M.– WHENEVER		← WATER! ALL THE WATER

Next Level Basic Tips:
24-7 COCKTAIL HOUR(S)

9:00 A.M.

Okay, you *never* have wine in the morning because if you're like me it makes you emotional and mean. Wine is reserved for nighttime so I don't wind up terrorizing anyone (usually my boyfriend or a friend). First thing in the morning is meant for caffeine, not cocktails. I'll have coffee or iced tea or a Diet Dr Pepper if I'm feeling "healthy." The only time I break this morning rule is if I'm going through a bad breakup, in which case I'll drink whatever I want first thing in the morning, whether it's a mimosa or a glass of wine from the night before. Once you're over the breakup you can go back to caffeine.

10:00 A.M.

An hour after waking you can move on to a Bloody Mary, mimosa, or Bellini—anything with champs or prosecco. This isn't the time for bottomless mimosas either—you have fourteen-plus hours left in your day, so just relax.

BRUNCH (11:00 A.M. TO 1:00 P.M.)

At brunch and/or lunch, continue with prosecco or an Aperol Spritz, because they're fucking fabulous. If you don't like those then I suggest something light and clean, like a Moscow Mule. Beer is good too, if you're a beer drinker. But I wouldn't stray too far from what you started with. This is not the time to throw down a bunch of martinis or shots. Trust me on this. Oh, and you have to eat at brunch. Don't try to be a skinny bitch and pick at your kale salad. Eat a burrito or a hamburger or some tacos, because you have a long day of drinking ahead.

HAPPY HOUR (5:00 P.M. TO 7:00 P.M.)

Okay, the rule here is: Stick to the same thing, folks. Be consistent or you'll feel sick and puke all over a limo. If you want margaritas, you better make sure margaritas are the only thing you're drinking that evening. You can maybe switch to vodka sodas later, since there's less sugar (and less hangover), but happy hour is when you set the course for the rest of the night, so choose wisely. Also try to have a glass of water for every drink you pound to help balance out the debauchery and keep you hydrated (you can thank me in the morning).

DINNER (8:00 P.M.)

This is when I break out the vino. Red wine is my absolute favorite, so I reserve it for dinner and afterward, in case I turn into a bitch. This way there is less time between me and bed, therefore less time for me to turn psycho. When choosing your dinner drink, the cardinal rule is: know thyself. Does whiskey make you fun, or evil? Does vodka make you want to dance, or throw a drink in someone's face? You have to go deep and figure yourself out before you commit to your dinner drink. Or you can always choose whatever goes with the food.

BED (11:00 P.M. TO WHENEVER)

It's time to trade in the cocktails for a hangover patch *and* a hangover pill. Also pound water. Ordering Taco Bell is always good too, and then the whole thing is over and you can pass out, sleep it off, and dream about your next Bellini.

While I've learned some things about handling myself, not passing out in public, and keeping hangovers at bay, I am not perfect (leave that to Meghan Markle). I still get too drunk sometimes, pass out, and then rally again. I still get hangovers. But I'm working on being better and finding that perfect balance between Meghan Markle and Barney Stinson.

Next Level Basic TAKEAWAY

There's an art to drinking like a Next Level Basic bitch, y'all. This is not amateur hour here! Do *not* throw up in limos, never drink wine in the morning, and don't forget to drink water throughout the night, which seems obvious but you would be surprised how many unenlightened drinkers forget this sacred rule. All of my rules might not apply to you—maybe you hate red wine or think Aperol Spritzes are revolting (and if so— *WTF?!*)—so adjust accordingly. But I know what I am talking about when it comes to this stuff. I have spent hours, weeks, and years perfecting it.

CHAPTER 16

A Foodie's Nightmare

Next Level Basic bitch Betty White once said that hot dogs and vodka are the secret to a long life, and I fully support her belief. In fact, I love hot dogs so much, I have an annual pass to Universal Studios, not because I like to bring my wand to Universal's Wizarding World of Harry Potter (which I do, BTW), but because *The Simpsons* section has the most delicious, basic AF hot dogs on the planet. Having basic taste in food probably makes most "foodies" shudder, but who says you can't be a foodie if you love dill pickle–flavored Lays potato chips? And who would *want* to be a foodie anyway if that were the case?

Living in LA and working as a server for years has exposed me to the worst of the worst kinds of food snobs. In my experience, there are two types: the ones who can only have "special" food but not for actual health reasons (like vegan, gluten-free, paleo, raw food, or keto). The second type might not have any restrictions, but they think they care more about food than the rest of us. I mean, how did the word "foodie" even come about? Everyone loves food. I've never met one person who is like, "Food? I'll pass. It's not my fave." No one in the history of the world has ever said that, so technically we are all foodies, because we all love to eat.

Foodies have this elitist attitude, like they have a rare, special, sophisticated, adventurous palate, while the rest of us just mow down anything in our path. It's so pretentious. A lot of their fancy food does taste good, but you know what else tastes good? Domino's pizza dipped in ranch. It's fucking phenomenal. I guarantee that the people who wait in line for two hours for a new restaurant that doesn't take reservations but only lets you, like, send a post-card to reserve a table (yes, there are pretentious restaurants in LA that do this) or wait outside for hours with a secret password are wishing they had some Domino's. I would never wait for hours to get into a restaurant. Brad Pitt could be in that restaurant, and I could know that he'd be at my table and that we were going to have a killer conversation, and I still would not wait for two hours. Chances are if you do wait that long, by the time you get in there that weird truffle caviar thing on top of a dot of foam mashed potato essence is not going to be as good as the local burger joint. You def won't be leaving hungry from there.

I will never say the words "I'm a foodie," but I crave food all the time, I think about it all the time, I plan my days around it, and I fantasize about it—so does that make me a fucking foodie? What qualifications do you need to have? When I worked at Sur, the worst were the people who would come in and say they were gluten-free, because half of them probably had no idea what gluten was, but they just heard that the hot girl in their Pilates class was gluten-free, so they decided that was their thing. The second worst were the people who would rudely complain about their meal, so then I'd bring them the same exact entrée and not change anything, and yet they were so appreciative and loved it and I'm like, "You've literally just wasted my time!" Are those foodies or just jerks? Either way, I don't want to be part of their club.

Do things like "farm to table" really matter that much? I get that it's probably more ethical and better for the planet, but it's such an elitist thing to demand to know exactly where your food came from and what it was fed. I think part of the farm-to-table foodie movement is that people want to eat food that looks pretty, not because they really love it better but because it looks better on Instagram than a bowl of mac 'n' cheese. You don't see people posting Hamburger Helper on Instagram, because it looks like vomit. I feel bad for Hamburger Helper because it's just not Instagram worthy. And don't get me started on size 0 models who constantly pose with giant bowls of pasta (with one little noodle coming out of their pouty mouth just so) or doughnuts and hashtag #foodie, like they actually eat carbs or any kind of food at all. I'm done with you people. No more looking hot and skinny AF in your Gucci loafers, posing with an uneaten hamburger. I'm starting a new movement. It's called #FUFoodies.

There was one time I opened myself up to vegan food, but it did not end well. We have a trans woman named Billie Lee on *Vanderpump* and the two of us became friends. She did my podcast because I wanted to tell her story, since she is such a strong, brave woman with an incredible story. And even though she was vegan and told me about it all the time, I liked her so I was like, "Okay, whatever." So during this time I got invited to the *Game of Thrones* premiere (which was going to be the best day of my life, since I am the #1 fan) but my producers wouldn't let me off work. On the show, Kristen and Billie Lee were hosting a vegan dinner event and the producers basically said that I had to be there. Like the professional I am, I went and filmed the episode and made jokes about the vegan food because that's the way I deal with life—I joke. But by the end of the night, I admitted . . . this shit is good. Not as good as *Game of Thrones* would have been, but still. The scene never aired, sadly, so no one heard me admit that I actually liked some vegan food.

So cut to a few days later, I found out that Billie was talking shit about me behind my back because I made fun of the vegan food. That's how PC we've gotten? I can't even make fun of food?

How does that hurt anyone's feelings if I joke about vegan cheese or jicama? I mean, Billie Lee didn't even make the food. Kristen Doute cooked and Billie was her sous chef! If I can't joke about vegan food, what can I joke about? Soon people who really love lampshades are going to be like, "NO JOKES ABOUT LAMP-SHADES!" The producers ended up cutting out the story line because it was too ridiculous to have drama about a few tofu egg rolls and some cashew cheese, and that was basically the beginning and the end of my vegan experience. *And* I had to miss *Game of Thrones* for all that.

So yes, I put ketchup on eggs, A.1. sauce on steak, and hot sauce on pretty much everything. It might offend some people, but who is the authority on which tastes are the right ones? My taste buds really enjoy hot sauce. Who decided that was wrong? Who decided that a plain piece of meat was sophisticated? Because ketchup comes in a plastic bottle from Ralphs and not a custom glass mason jar made by monks? Please. If anyone can be a food authority, then I officially declare a new Next Level Basic version of the basic food groups:

Next Level Basic FOOD GROUPS

GOAT-CHEESE BALLS

This obsession of mine started at Sur. I feel like goat-cheese balls are a hidden gem and I'm salivating like a wolf thinking about them. These should be at the top of any Next Level Basic bitch's food pyramid.

ICEBERG, CHEDDAR, AND RANCH SALAD

This is so basic and also technically gross but . . . is there anything more delicious? I mean, tons of foods are technically gross but "foodies" love them: salmon eggs, foie gras, head cheese (which is not cheese at all but meat jelly from a cow's or pig's head, GTFO). The key to this food group is that you have to use good ranch (more on my ranch obsession in this chapter). Otherwise, you're just eating a head of lettuce.

MAC 'N' CHEESE *FROM A BOX*

I am not talking fancy baked truffle mac 'n' cheese. I mean Kraft or Annie's. Even better if the macaroni is in the shape of something special, like if there's a new Marvel movie coming out and it's superhero shapes or if it's Easter and you get bunny rabbit shapes. This isn't just a cutesy thing—it's practical. With shapes, the powdered cheese gets caught in all the little holes and crevices, so it makes every bite more delicious. Unlike restaurant mac 'n' cheese, with a box you can personalize your pasta: you can use hot sauce; you can make it soupy or creamy, depending on your mood. This food group is also best consumed late at night right before you pass out.

PIZZA AND RANCH

This combo is always amazing. Even pizza from Chuck E. Cheese's is still good, even though it's not wood-fired and organic with cremini mushrooms on top. Low-rent pizzas may not be the most elegant, but they're still going to taste good in your mouth. In fact, for me, even better. Add ranch for dipping and the food group is complete.

TACO BELL WITH FIRE SAUCE

This is another late-night food group (which is also good for you when you're totes hungover the next day). I order one of everything from Taco Bell so I can dip it in the fire sauce and take one bite of each thing, like a fast-food smorgasbord. It's wasteful I know, but don't judge.

CHEESE

If there is one food group I could not give up it would be dairy. I can give up sugar and carbs and meat if I *had* to, but cheese? I could never. I want to do one of those blood-type tests to see what foods work best for me but I'm too scared to do it because I'm afraid they're going to tell me I shouldn't have dairy. I have never met a cheese I didn't like, and I have no shame in the cheese game. The Europeans know what's up. I would have my wedding cake made of cheese if I could, and for the record, sliced American cheese is the most underrated food on the planet. Yep, I said it. I dare any "foodie" to try it and disagree. As a side note, there have been some articles written about how millennials are ruining American cheese by shunning processed food, and I have never been more ashamed to be a millennial.

HOT SAUCE

I know this is not technically a "food," but I think about what hot sauce I'm in the mood for before I even think of the actual food I want. Every meal I choose is based on what hot sauce I'm craving, so therefore it belongs on the pyramid. I'll use sriracha for any Asian food (Thai, Chinese, or sushi). I also use it on eggs, mac 'n' cheese, and sometimes even pizza. Cholula is for anything Mexican (plus eggs and mac 'n' cheese). Tabasco and Frank's are the kings of breakfast hot sauce (plus mac 'n' cheese and eggs).

Next Level Basic TAKEAWAY

Two words: Hot dogs. Also: Mac 'n' cheese. Hot sauce. Goat-cheese balls. We are *all* foodies, so do not let anyone make you feel less than because you would rather dine on Shake 'n Bake potatoes than truffle celery root puree with gold-flecked sea salt sprinkled on top. Own your basic food choices. I do, and it makes my life so much more fulfilling to embrace my midnight mac 'n' cheese and pizza with ranch instead of pretending I like charred kale. I mean, I'll eat kale here and there because I want to be at least a little healthy, but I don't have to pretend I *adore* the stuff. Life is too short.

Next Level Basic Map:
BEST HOT DOGS ON THE PLANET

Like goat-cheese balls and hot sauce, I am obsessed with hot dogs. Not alligator-meat sausage with organic buns or boar sausage made with truffle relish—just basic AF, simple hot dogs. I have tried hot dogs from California to France and back again, and if someone started an international tour based on the best hot dog spots in the world, I could for sure lead that tour. So based on my careful research over the years, I present to you . . .

THE BEST HOT DOGS ON THE PLANET
(YOU'RE WELCOME)

UNIVERSAL STUDIOS, LOS ANGELES, CALIFORNIA, USA: Get them at Suds McDuff's Hot Dog House. Simple, uncomplicated, and perfectly sized. Your only condiment options are ketchup, mustard, and relish. It's like hot dogs for five-year-olds and I LOVE IT.

DODGER STADIUM, LOS ANGELES, CALIFORNIA, USA: Yes, "Dodger Dogs" are a thing and you can get these ten-inch bundles of joy grilled or steamed. It takes a lot to get me to a sports event, and Dodger Dogs are literally the only reason I've ever gone to a baseball game.

HOT DOG CARTS: How do they always show up at exactly the right time? Namely at, like, 2:00 a.m. And they're so quick and efficient! I always wonder how they hold so many different condiments in such a small portable space. Ketchup, mustard, relish, hot sauce, chopped onions, mayo, hot peppers, sauerkraut, cheese, chili. If you're a true "foodie," you know what I'm talking about here, specifically:

BOURBON STREET, NEW ORLEANS, LOUISIANA, USA: Probably where my love of basic hot dogs began. Those hot dog carts saved my life plenty of times as a young, inexperienced drinker.

ANY STREET IN NEW YORK CITY, NEW YORK, USA: I feel like this needs no explanation.

MCDONALD'S, PARIS, FRANCE: "Le P'tit Hot Dog." Yes, a fancy-ass name for a hot dog at a Parisian McDonald's, and yes, I went to Paris and walked my ass into a McDonald's because I just had to try it. They're tiny, cute, tasty . . . a lovely snack after a long day of sightseeing. Especially when you've had way too many charcuterie boards.

THE 7-ELEVEN AT THE COPENHAGEN AIRPORT, COPENHAGEN, DENMARK: Okay, bear with me, but their hot dogs are strange (yet delicious) AF. Apparently, they are called "Czech-style hot dogs." If I try to explain it I'll sound like a sexual predator with a thing for hot dogs, so instead I'll quote the always trusty Wikipedia, which explains it like this: "Rather than slicing the bun in half and placing the sausage into the resultant cleavage, the top of the bun (*rohlík*) is cut off, with a hole punched into the softer inside of the bun where condiments and then the sausage is placed, similar to the Ketwurst." Basically, you squirt the ketchup and mustard in the hole and then stick the sausage in. It's delicious, I swear.

PINK'S HOT DOGS, LOS ANGELES, CALIFORNIA, USA: While my personal hot dog preference is simple and basic, I still very much appreciate hot dogs with a creative flair. Pink's is a Hollywood landmark that has an endless line outside and endless amounts of hot dog choices. Just google the menu and you'll understand. Also, I aspire to have a hot dog at Pink's named after me one day (it would be my version of an Academy Award). And that hot dog would be as basic as it comes.

"ROLLING KITCHENS" FOOD TRUCK FESTIVAL, AMSTERDAM, NETHER-LANDS: Why is it that everything tastes better when it comes from a food truck? Has this been scientifically proven yet? All I know is that when I was in Amsterdam, I went to this festival and the hot dog truck was NEXT LEVEL BASIC.

TOP RANCH DRESSINGS OF ALL TIME

Anyone who watches *Vanderpump* or follows me on social media knows that I love ranch dressing. It's an underrated condiment that every basic bitch should embrace and respect, no questions asked. I've spent (most of) my life searching for the best ranch dressings on the planet. I know exactly why they're so amazing, and what you can eat them with—pizza, hot wings (with extra hot sauce), goat-cheese balls (sometimes) . . .

Just think of me as your ranch sommelier.

In case you think ranch is just some dumb condiment, you should know that it was invented by a plumber named Steve in 1949. He was working in a remote part of Alaska, so he had plenty of time to perfect his buttermilk-dressing recipe. A few years later he opened a dude ranch called—yep—Hidden Valley Ranch, and they served Steve's secret recipe to customers. It became so popular that Steve and his wife sold it to Clorox for eight million bucks. The company sells like $450 million worth of ranch a year now, so maybe Steve should have haggled, but then again, he made millions off a ranch-dressing recipe that he made up in the backwoods of Alaska, so . . . he won because he retired a wealthy, world-famous ranch dressing mogul.

If you, too, are ready to embrace this basic AF, delicious condiment that sometimes gets shoved aside for aioli or vegan tahini dip, I have put my years of intense research to use and compiled a list of the ranch dressings that every Next Level Basic bitch needs in her life, now. I dare you to go on a ranch road trip and try them all in the next six months, and use the handy map below as your guide.

Top Ranch Dressings of All Time

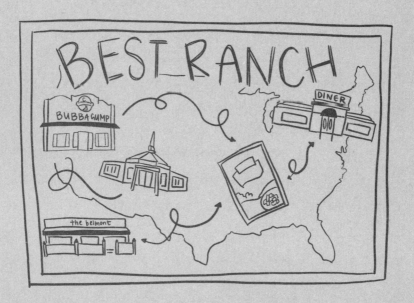

HOMEMADE RANCH MADE WITH THE HIDDEN VALLEY PACKET: This 100 percent tops any store-bought or restaurant made ranch. What kind of crack are they putting in this seasoning? Major plus side to this one—you can tailor the consistency to your taste. Or make it healthier by subbing Greek yogurt for mayo. Growing up, I would get so flipping excited when my mom would say it was salad night, because that meant heaps of homemade ranch. And yes, we had salad night.

THE RANCH AT BUBBA GUMP SHRIMP COMPANY: This one might be surprising but it's true. I legitimately dream about the Bubba Gump Shrimp chain restaurants. My subconscious goes there all the time. I personally frequent the Universal CityWalk location because feeling like a tourist legit excites me. No, I do not go to Bubba Gump for the seafood. I basically order some iceberg lettuce, cheddar cheese, and ranch. You can skip the Bubba Gump shrimp and go straight for the ranch. Just eat it with a spoon if you want. I won't judge.

JACK IN THE BOX BUTTERMILK HOUSE SAUCE: Oh, those little packets of joy. I refuse to eat fast food without it. I mean, it's so good that a fight broke out in 2013 at a Washington location because a man couldn't get a third packet of ranch for free. I can't say I blame him; ranch is serious freaking business.

RANCH DRESSING AT DINERS: For realzies, why is it that every single diner across America has awesome ranch? I feel like there's this diner cult, where all the employees have been shown the recipe and sworn to secrecy. I want in on this cult. If you're in it and you're reading this, please contact me ASAP. I will join, no questions asked.

THE RANCH AT THE BELMONT, WEST HOLLYWOOD, CALIFORNIA: Okay, this one is real specific because this isn't a chain restaurant, but whatevs. The Belmont is to me what Central Perk was to *Friends*. I'm always there; my friends are always there. It's our hub. And now as I'm writing this I'm wondering if I made it our hub because of their ranch. It's perfect. Just the right amount of dill, with a balanced consistency. If you're traveling to Los Angeles, this should be at the top of your list, right up there with the Hollywood sign and the beach. Maybe even above the beach.

MARIE'S: As far as bottled ranch dressings go, this is my fave. Store-bought ranch is always risky, but if you're a true lover of the ranch arts, you're safe with this one. That Marie just got it right. BTW, who *is* Marie? I'd like to meet her and invite her to the ranch-dressing diner cult. (Side note: If you don't like a thick consistency, I would recommend adding a bit of store-bought yogurt-based ranch dressing to water it down a little . . . you're welcome).

THE RANCH AT PAPAGAYOS IN LAKE ARROWHEAD, CALIFORNIA: Another obscure mention, I know, but think of this list as a ranch travelogue that'll inspire you to go on vacation—and eat ranch. The population of Lake Arrowhead is, like, fifteen, and I've spent a lot of time there because after Hurricane Katrina we lost our home, and my mom took my siblings and me across the country to live in Lake Arrowhead. There are fewer than ten restaurants in this town (give or take), but the Mexican joint Papagayos knows what's up when it comes to ranch. Taco salad with three sides of ranch? Yes, please. I like to be adventurous with my ranch, and I also love a good theme, so at this place, I add Cholula hot sauce. It's the bomb.

HONORABLE MENTION: Hidden Valley bottle: Okay, this one is just getting an honorable mention because Hidden Valley is the ruler of ranches. I mean, I have a rhinestone-bedazzled Hidden Valley bottle (for real) and I read that they released $35,000 *diamond-encrusted* bottles in honor of Prince Harry marrying an American. LIKE WHAT??? Are people actually in the market for eighteen-karat white gold ranch bottles trimmed with diamonds and sapphires? I mean, I guess I would be, but I don't even have central AC, so one thing at a time. Another reason this made the list? It's Kristen Doute's absolute fave ranch, and she'd take a bullet for it, so that's gotta mean something.

BONUS SECTION:
HOW RANCH CEMENTS FRIENDSHIPS

Ranch is so basic that it can truly be life changing. If someone hates it, then I seriously question our relationship. And if someone uses ranch to show me how much they love me—I know that friendship is for life.

You know what kind of friend someone is when they are willing to drink a cup of ranch for you. Even I have my ranch limits, but Katie Maloney was once in New York and she just happened upon a ranch pop-up. (Like, how does one get that lucky?) She saw that they were giving away merch and asked how she could get something, *anything*, with ranch on it. The answer? Drink a full cup of ranch as if it were a large shot of tequila. She did it, and I am now the proud owner of a "Legalize Ranch" baseball cap. That is truly taking basic bitch friendship to the next level.

One of my best friends made me a ranch fountain for my twenty-ninth birthday party. She made vats of it in her apartment and bought a fondue fountain online, and brought it all to my murder-themed birthday party. The whole place was decorated like a haunted house and we were all dressed like dead people, eating ranch out of a giant metal fondue fountain. Shout-out to Rachael O'Brien for that one.

Kristen Doute once made two different homemade ranches, one vegan and one regular. Then she made me do a blind taste test. Sadly, I chose the vegan one. I know, I'm so ashamed.

CHAPTER 17

What's Your Sign?

I am one hundred percent as basic as it gets when it comes to astrology. I don't live or die by it, but I do, without fail, turn to the zodiac during major turning points in my life, like when I start dating someone and I need to see if we're truly compatible. I also turn to astrology when I'm going through a breakup to find out WTF went wrong and to see if we were always destined to implode. It comforts me because it makes me feel like it wasn't *me* who was the problem—it was just destiny. Astrology helps you discover that some dude didn't ghost you because he met a twenty-two-year-old bikini model; he ghosted you because you're an Aries and he's a Virgo and it was written in the stars that it would never work out! And then you can move on.

Besides dating and relationships, I also turn to astrology when I want to validate things about myself and come up with excuses for the way I act. For example, I'm a Cancer, and Cancers are crabs that have a hard outer shell, but they're actually the most sensitive sign in the zodiac. So I can't help it—being sensitive is in my nature. I also use my zodiac sign as an excuse for being a homebody, because that's also "written in the stars." For Cancers, our homes are our sanctuaries. We like to feel safe and comfortable. So every time my boyfriend, Beau, is like, "Let's stay out longer!" I'm like, "No, I'm a Cancer, we're going home . . ." He can't argue with that, so here's a pro tip: using the traits of your zodiac sign is a pretty convenient way to get people to do what you want.

I think everyone is inherently narcissistic to a certain degree, and we like to learn about ourselves and feel like there's some sort of destiny for each of us. Most basic bitches have memorized the traits of their sign and the traits of anyone they've ever dated. I own several astrology books (including a "sextrology" book that helps you find your most sexually compatible signs), but I don't read daily horoscopes that say things like *There will be a shift today and you will find love,* because there is no way that every single Cancer out there or every single Gemini is going through the same experiences. I also don't believe the articles at the end of a magazine that say, *These are the types of earrings you should buy if you're a Scorpio!* I mean, does every single Scorpio have the same taste in jewelry? I don't think so. I like to read things about my personality, but when it comes to the day-to-day predictions, I'm an astrology skeptic.

Besides my collection of astrology books, I have had a bunch of readings over the years. I've always been into tarot and the occult, and having my astrological reading done by a professional (which is based on the time, place, and date of your birth) is just fun, and is something every basic bitch should try. They figure out the alignment of the planets at the exact moment and place of your birth, use a bunch of signs and symbols to decipher everything, and then tell you things like what you're meant to do in life, what kind of person you're destined to marry, or when a major turning point might happen. Sometimes it's eerily similar to what's happening in your life, and sometimes it's kind of BS. But it's always fun. If you're struggling to find the perfect gift for the basic bitch in your life, I highly recommend an astrology reading as a present.

Like I said, I love reading about astrology because it validates some of my behaviors. Besides being extremely sensitive, we have strong survival instincts; we're protective of those we care about and of ourselves. That said, Cancers are also very private, and I share my life with the world for a living so . . . that doesn't make a whole lot of sense. But at times I can be extremely introverted. I guess because I'm on a reality show and I have a podcast where I let it all out, I'm pretty selective about who I actually share my life with, so I guess that's Cancer*ish*. I also have the Cancer trait of loving history, which I think explains my love of antiques, cemeteries, and old homes.

You would never find me living in a brand-new McMansion, for example. As for the Cancer weaknesses, I am definitely: changeable, lazy, overly sensitive, and manipulative (at times). I can be moody AF. But I can't help it—it's written in the stars.

On *Vanderpump*, Ariana Madix did not like me for *years*, and yet we have the same birthday! I never understood it because we had never gotten in a fight and nothing had ever happened between us—she just had a problem with me. I was so confused by it—I mean, am I *that* annoying? Now we're friends, but it took a good six years for her to realize that I'm not so bad. But (maybe because we share a birthday and a sign) I see similarities between us all the time. I've tried to explain to her that we are both total Cancers: we both have an intense interest in the occult; we're both totally moody; we're secretly sensitive but pretend we're hard-core; we're both superprotective of our friends (which is why we butted heads because we were both protecting different people). Now we send each other basic bitch Instagram posts like *How you know you're a Cancer* . . . or *Things that Cancers love* memes. She recently sent me a meme that listed a bunch of traits we both share, like:

Homebody

Supports other people's chaos (which is hysterical because that's exactly what we do on reality TV)

Moody and emotional

Vivid childhood memories

Social anxiety (which we both get all the time)

Holds grudges

Likes animals more than humans (this is 100% true)

Serial monogamist

Loves HGTV (random, but true)

Good emotional memory

Cries when yelled at

Drinks tea

Empathizes with film protagonists

Obviously there are plenty of Cancers out there who drink coffee and who hate HGTV, but the point of astrology is that some of this stuff *is* true, and it helps you bond with other people who might share your traits, or who might always also date Leos who love attention and hate monogamy. I'm not an astrology expert, but I have read enough about it and have had enough real-life experiences to create a simple guide, which might be a good primer as you start to get into this stuff.

Next Level Basic GUIDE TO THE ZODIAC

ARIES: They totally had school spirit in high school. And I bet they all love organizing karaoke nights.

TAURUS: Totes want to have a Taurus around in a zombie apocalypse. They. Get. Shit. Done.

GEMINI: I don't know . . . these fuckers scare the shit out of me. Maybe it's because their symbol is the twins, or maybe it's because so many actors in LA are Geminis. Or maybe it's written in the stars that Cancers and Geminis don't get each other. Who knows.

CANCER: Feeling like you want to stay in, be a recluse, order Postmates, and actually Netflix and chill in the literal sense? Then you want to date a Cancer.

LEO: Napoleon Bonaparte and Madonna were/are Leos. I'd totally take a confidence class from a Leo.

VIRGO: I would definitely trust a Virgo to plan out a detailed schedule of my whole future, and I would actually follow it. They are perfectionists.

LIBRA: I would totally want a Libra as a judge if I was accused of something I didn't do. These folks love to see both sides and are fair AF.

SCORPIO: Okay, I always hear that Scorpios are the best in bed, but I've never been with one, so who the heck knows? Maybe you do?

SAGITTARIUS: Sagittarius peeps are *the* best travel buddies. If you don't have one in your orbit, go find one and then plan a trip.

CAPRICORN: Much like Virgos, I want a group of Capricorns to come organize my closet.

AQUARIUS: You definitely want to take an Aquarius with you if you're going to Coachella. They're social, fun, and would never ditch you to go home and sleep.

PISCES: I feel like I'd want an artsy Pisces to paint me like Leo did with Rose in *Titanic*. #Goals.

I'm not saying this stuff is gospel, but at the very least it might entertain you for a few hours on a boring Sunday. And maybe it will help you discover some things about yourself. Just think of it as one step on the Next Level Basic road to enlightenment.

Next Level Basic TAKEAWAY

Astrology does the same thing that religion does for some people. It makes you feel like there is some sort of destiny and we're not just here on the earth walking around with no purpose. As silly as it seems, it gives meaning to life by making you think that there is something bigger out there, and that you are connected to all these other people because you love home-decorating shows or hate caffeine. And I admit, astrology also appeals to my vanity by validating some of the things I do. And if nothing else, it's a good way to bond with people at bars.

CHAPTER 18

Hashtag Namaste

We're living in the age of Goop, so getting your vagina steam-cleaned and eating clay or getting blood facials is pretty standard in some circles. But what you may have realized by now (since I consider boxed mac 'n' cheese a food group) is that by nature I am not a wellness-type person. My idea of wellness is a *90 Day Fiancé* marathon with me lounging on my couch. But I grew up with a best friend in New Orleans (shout-out to Sheena Mannina again) who all throughout high school was super into spas and cleanses. She always said she wanted to own a spa, whereas I was like, *Well, one day I want to move to LA and work in the entertainment industry.* And we accomplished both of those things. Sheena not only owns a juice bar called

Raw Republic in New Orleans but she also has a wellness center called the Space. And yet we are somehow still friends.

Because Sheena is the exact opposite of me in every single way, I constantly learn about (and try) wellness things I would never otherwise know. I am not part of the LA crowd that's like, "What's the next best thing? Oh, a vampire facial where Kim Kardashian is wiping blood all over her face! Perfect!" I mean, I love murder and mayhem, so you would think I'd be into that, but are you really going to tell me that wiping your own blood on your face is good for your skin? No, thank you. So I cannot get behind the blood facial, and I cannot tolerate anything that has to do with chanting. Yes, I've done a sound bath because Sheena was visiting me in LA and she wanted me to try it, but once people start doing weird things with their voices I become that immature human being in the meditation class who keeps one eye open and totally judges everyone around me. Chanting makes me feel weird, and I get chills, which is probably not the effect it's supposed to have.

That said, there are wellness things that sound not so horrible to me. For instance, I want to try this beer bath in the Czech Republic that's supposed to be good for your skin and hair, and I imagine you can do it and get hammered at the same time. Why don't we have those in the United States? I've also always been interested in sensory deprivation tanks, but I'm scared to try it. You get in a pitch-black, silent tank and just float. I feel like it would be the scariest thing I could ever do because I'd get claustrophobic. What if the person who puts me in the tank watches *Vanderpump Rules* and I'm her least favorite character and she locks me in there and I die? That would suck. "Stassi died in an isolation tank, alone, in the dark." So I'm thinking I'll never do it.

Thanks to Sheena, I've done the normal things, like mud baths and acupuncture and fish spas, where the fish give you a pedicure. I've gone back and forth between a steam room and a cold pool. I've done energy work. I tried a (traumatic) colonic. What I would never do, even for $5 million, is one of those snail spas in Tokyo where they put giant living snails all over your face. I would also never do the snake massage in Israel, and most definitely not the python massage in the Philippines. It's a thing. Google it.

Sheena doesn't try to lure me into snake or snail wellness experiences, but she does con me (or gently coax me) into trying things I would never do on my own. Partly because wellness centers have totally culty vibes (sorry, Sheena). Everyone is oddly calm and happy, and their whole lives are about wellness, and they want you to join them and see their side. At Sheena's wellness center, they do cupping (you know, the thing Gwyneth Paltrow and all the Olympians like Michael Phelps do that leaves those round red marks all over their backs). Regular cupping is when they apply heated glass cups to your skin, which creates a suction that stimulates energy flow. At her spa, it's a "wet cupping" called hijama. It's like medicinal bleeding (which does not sound as relaxing as drinking a glass of wine on your couch). Blood is drawn by suction from a small incision on the back of your neck, which surprisingly doesn't hurt. When I did it, the woman explained that depending on your mental and emotional and physical health, everyone's blood looks different. Sometimes it's lighter or darker, thicker or thinner. Sometimes there's a lot, and sometimes a little. But there is no explanation for what my blood did that day.

Soon after she started the hijama process, the woman doing the cupping just said, "Oh" in a weird tone. And I was like, "What do you mean, *Oh*?" Then she told me my blood was bubbling and that she had never seen that happen before. *Bubbling?* Like a cauldron or something? Did that mean I was evil? Was I possessed by some demon? Why was my blood bubbling? I've tried googling it and I can't find anything that explains it. I did feel relaxed after, but it must mean something deeper. Maybe in this situation, though, ignorance is bliss?

Despite the fact that I have witch blood and I hate chanting, I'm going to share some wellness experiences that might help you decide whether you want to do some energy work or have a hose stuck up your butt, all in the name of health.

Next Level Basic Tips:
BASIC WELLNESS

KOREAN SPAS

At the ones I've been to, they force you to get naked and then they scrub you down, contorting your body in a big wash room in front of a bunch of strangers to get to every last crevice. You feel like you're in *The Walking Dead* and you need to be quarantined to get the disease off you. I can scrub myself down with a loofah at home, thank you very much. I don't enjoy having a stranger scrub off my spray tan in front of strangers, but the spa part is nice.

ENERGY WORK

I waver between believing and not believing in this. Someone puts crystals on your body and uses their hands to do energy healing. There have been a few times where I started to cry during a treatment, but I think it's because I was going through a breakup or maybe I just felt uncomfortable. During these sessions, all I can think about is where I'm going to have dinner or what I want to wear next. Does it work? I don't know. But it gives me space to think about food and clothing without distractions, so that's relaxing.

ALIEN READINGS

I learned about these from Sheena, of course. She gets alien readings to find out what kind of alien energy is around her or what or who her alien ancestors are. I love the idea of aliens, and I definitely believe in them. Do I think they're shape-shifters walking around in our government? I don't know, but anything is possible. I've never gotten one of these, but I'm open to it.

WITCH SESSIONS

Okay. I have a bad habit of having late-night temper tantrums and freak-outs, and I can't control myself and it's upsetting. I've gone to therapy, but it was inconclusive. I wanted to find out why this was happening, so I went to this witch in Los Angeles, who came from a line of Wiccan women. I got to her house downtown and sat in a circle with an altar and everything, and it was the most intense scene I have ever filmed in the history of all the reality shows I have done. I sobbed, I felt like I was in a trance, it was insane. The witch told me to confront the demon that lived inside of me and made me act crazy, and I could only describe this demon as a heavy black cloud. Then she told me to speak to this demon and change it into something that wasn't so scary. So, no joke, I started imagining this cloud as the white puffy cloud from the *Mario Kart* video game, which is the most innocent-looking thing you can imagine. After the trance, the witch had me write a letter to myself, the demon, and anyone I felt I had let down. Then I had to make an altar to the *Mario*

Kart cloud, so that whenever I feel myself getting anxious I can center myself and turn the dark cloud into something innocent. After the experience, I was drained for a week. So now I believe in aliens *and* witches.

COLONIC

I'll never let Sheena forget this awful experience, which was much scarier than hanging out with a witch. When Sheena visits me in LA her idea of fun is going to wellness centers. She chooses my treatment and I usually trust her. But this time when we got there I asked what she signed me up for, and she laughed and said a colonic. I protested, but in a very Zen way she convinced me to have a hose shoved up my butt. You're in a room with a squatty potty and you lay down and they stick a hose up your ass and pump you full of water. They have mirrors on the ceiling so you can crane your neck to look up and watch if you want. It felt like I took four hundred laxatives and that I was being pumped full of water. The woman doing the colonic massaged my stomach and I felt like I was going to die. Then she wanted to have a therapy session, asking me what's going on in my life. How could I possibly answer that while there's a hose up my butt? Then she explained that I couldn't drink for forty-eight hours and I was like . . . that's funny. Afterward, I went straight to the bar and had a glass of organic wine, and let me tell you, I was like a newborn baby after I drank that wine. I was hammered. If you get colonics regularly you might save money on alcohol, which is the only reason it is on this list. Otherwise I'd say just eat fiber and hope for the best.

So even after all of this, I still have no idea what "balance" means. I'm still trying to figure that out. I always tell Sheena I'm never going to be Zen like she is, but she tells me that I am—and that I just don't know it. Sheena and her coworkers also think I'm some sort of healer-type personality, but I think I fit more with the "destroyers." I destroy bottles of wine; I destroy pizzas; I destroy hot dogs. In my mind, anything that makes you happy and relaxed is positive, which is why binge-watching reality shows is my way of being balanced and centered. So to each their freaking own—that's a wellness mantra I can get behind.

Next Level Basic TAKEAWAY

You will never catch me chanting (well, at least I don't think so), but I have learned to open myself up to some basic enlightenment thanks to spas, cupping, and Los Angeles–based witches. Enlightenment doesn't have to be torture, like a thirty-day fast where you deprive yourself of all joy in an attempt to find nirvana or whatever. It can actually be fun, but you might have to try a few (horrible) things like colonics to find the path that works for you.

CHAPTER 19

Basic Mistakes

So maybe by now you consider me an authority on hot dogs, #OOTDs, and musical theater. But like I said, I'm not an authority on life in general (unless mac 'n' cheese = life, which it *kind of* is). Still, one thing I have learned is that you can't grow and become enlightened as a basic bitch unless you admit to and learn from the dumb things you do. And we *all* do dumb stuff— even Dame Judi Dench. I've said things on camera and via social media and my podcast that caused controversy, offended people, and taught me that we all screw up, and we can all be basic (or serious) assholes at times. The point is to embrace your fuckups because that's the only way you can take your basicness (and your true self) to the next level.

Over the last few years I have been embarrassed about so many things I have said and done, it makes me cringe. I wish I could wipe my mistakes away as easily as I can delete an Insta post, but we all know that's not possible. The first time I truly felt like I hurt people was pretty far into *Vanderpump*. I was talking about the Academy Awards on my podcast and I brought up the fact that everyone's speech had to do with politics or Black Lives Matter or gender issues, and I remember being like *Why is everything political?* I said that when I watch the Oscars I want to forget about all those problems and not have to watch actors make speeches about them. After the podcast, I realized that my comments made so many people feel underappreciated and unheard. I apologized and admitted that I was ignorant, so I read listeners' emails and tried to educate myself about the issues and how people felt.

I was ignorant because I am a privileged white girl who grew up without much adversity, so who the eff am I to make a comment about anything? I have no idea what it's like for someone else who faces adversity. The whole thing made me realize that for better or worse, what I say has an effect. It's hard to recognize that when you're just on a reality show, because you just think: *Who am I? I'm not a role model; I do shots and fight with people on camera as a job.* But at that moment I realized my opinion did affect people, and it was scary, more than anything else. It also made me realize that I am super ignorant about so many things and unaware and it has motivated me to want to sit and listen and learn from what everyone's different opinions are, and to be careful about how I say something. I'll always be opinionated, but I don't want to be that person who is like, "Whatever—I tell it like it is so deal with it!" There's a level of respect that everyone deserves, so I don't have the right to say whatever I want. That was a hard pill to swallow.

The next mistake was in 2017 when the #MeToo movement came about. I did an hour-long podcast episode where I was challenging things that were being said because it felt like anyone could come out and tweet that someone did something to them, and immediately that person would be fired without anything going through the court system. I wanted to start a dialogue about that, and looking back I did it in the wrong way. It sounded like I was shaming victims, which makes me incredibly sad, because that's so sacred and personal and I would never want anyone to think I was shaming them. I was saying there should be a system in place, and to be honest I still struggle with it. I am a feminist and I love strong women, and I was trying to work out my own thoughts about the issues, and I happened to do it very publicly, and maybe not in the most enlightened way.

Within two hours of that podcast being live, 75 percent of my sponsors fired me. Some sponsors did it publicly through social media, to use what I was going through to further themselves. I didn't have time to defend myself before it all blew up, and I never want anyone to think I am someone who doesn't care about what others are going through. I learned that unless I have researched the subject and learned as much as I can about it, I probably shouldn't say anything at all. That doesn't mean you can't be outspoken, but it does mean you shouldn't just go off on issues without educating yourself from all sides.

Oh, but wait—there's more! My next mistake happened because of an #OOTD. I'll start by saying that like many Southerners, I love monograms. Unfortunately, my initials happen to be SS (like Nazi soldiers), and it took me a while to get the correlation. I had my initials monogrammed onto a military-style coat of mine that I wore during a trip to Europe, and my friends pointed out that walking around Europe with "SS" on my jacket wasn't the greatest fashion statement. It didn't help that the initials were also on my keychain and necklace. So, the term "Nazi chic" became a joke between me and my friends, which we never intended to be offensive in any way. But then I went and posted an OOTD in an outfit with a monogram and I captioned it "Nazi chic." Obviously, not a smart move, since I now realize it looked like I was glorifying Nazism.

After that I lost every single sponsor, so it was basically like starting over. I have never cried so hard. I cried so hard that my nose exploded with blood and it looked like I had murdered someone in my bedroom. I know now that the things I said and wrote were and are so insensitive, and after the nose-exploding-in-blood incident, I learned to listen to other people, because that's the only way I can be better, as a true Next Level Basic bitch.

The wrong way to deal with basic mistakes is to try to justify them or get defensive, because you're cutting yourself off from trying to see the other side. I can't deny that I said and did things I regret. I need to acknowledge what I did because people who got hurt are owed that. But what I can do is just promise to try to be better. Really the true key to embracing your fuckups is alcohol. Just kidding. It takes every ounce of humility (whether it happens publicly or not) to acknowledge that you're wrong, but for the sake of being a decent human being, embracing it is the only thing you can do. You deal with the cold sweats and sleep in the bed you made and deal with it.

I want to be a well-rounded basic bitch and educate myself by trying to understand the different sides to every story. As trivial as talking about embracing your basic bitch may be, maybe it's my way of contributing to society in a positive way, by helping people be themselves, no matter what the haters say. Because when you feel wholly yourself, that's when we are our happiest. We are not all blessed with the skills to cure diseases or really make a difference in monumental ways. I know my strengths, and one is encouraging us to laugh at ourselves, not take ourselves too seriously, and to talk about how being a basic bitch isn't a bad thing—it's an awesome thing. We should all strive to live every single day as our truest selves, obviously as long as we are not hurting or murdering people (or making major mistakes by insulting hundreds or thousands of people).

So, my basic bitches, I'll leave you with this: think of times you have felt your happiest and make a list of them, and then take some time to think about why you were happy. Yes, sometimes it'll be because you were with loved ones, or it was your twenty-first birthday, or your son was born, but a lot of them will be simply because you were yourself and you were not having to pretend to be a foodie who despises hot dogs, or a TV hater who would never watch the *Kardashians* (even though you watch it on the reg). Look to those moments and aspire to keep those moments going . . . and that's what makes you an enlightened Next Level Basic bitch badass.

Next Level Basic TAKEAWAY

To truly become a Next Level Basic bitch, you have to be willing to admit your mistakes, take responsibility, and learn from them so you don't keep acting like a jerk, whether it's on social media or in real life. As much as I would love to just erase the major mistakes I've made and pretend they never happened, I've tried to take them to heart and figure out where I went wrong, and apologize to anyone I hurt along the way. I'm all about speaking your mind and owning who you are, but you have to embrace the major fuckups along the way, because that's how you take your basicness to the next level and become the best basic bitch you can possibly be.

Acknowledgments

Alrighty, enough about me. . . .

This all started with my parents, so if you didn't like this book, you can blame them. Thank you, Mom and Dad, for constantly telling me that I could do anything I put my mind to. Cliché? Yes. But 100 percent true. I mean, if they hadn't told me every day how special I was, there is a good chance I could've ended up under a freeway overpass or, like, on *Hoarders* or something. Dad, seriously seriously seriously thank you for paying for my expensive-ass college tuition *even* after I told you I was going to be an English major. I mean, that's love, support, and acceptance right there.

Now for the people who took a chance on me as a destitute SURver and put me on a show, because let's be honest, would this book have been published if I wasn't on *Vanderpump Rules*? Probz not. The platform I have been given by the Bravo network and Evolution Media has gotten me here, and I am forever grateful for that. Lisa Vanderpump, you have been such an inspiration to watch and be around. Your work ethic is like none other, you have truly mastered the art of doing it all, and your jewelry collection is *phenom*. Andy Cohen, thank you for taking one look at our restaurant photo and telling us to go for it. Our *VPR* creators, Alex Baskin and Douglas Ross, bless you both. (Also, thanks for letting me come back for season four, *totes* appreciative.) Our producers, Bill Langworthy, John Carr, Jeremiah Smith, Erin Foye—and everyone who has worked on *Vanderpump Rules*. You guys are family. Being able to come back to the same team year after year has been one of the best parts of doing the show, and has given me the ability to be so open. Everyone at Bravo—Frances Berwick, Ryan Flynn, Shari Levine, Jerry Leo—you all allowing me to skinny-dip across everyone's TV screens has gotten me here.

I can't tell you how long my publicist, Emily Clay Hessel, has been trying to get me to write a book. I think it's been four years now? Emily, you have the sweetest soul (teach me), and your constant motivation has helped me more than you could ever know.

I have a badass team of women around me. Last year when I met with Kendall Ostrow and Brandi Bowles at UTA, I finally felt *home*. You girls just got me, and I knew you two were the perfect pair to have on my side. You guys are truly Next Level Basic *bawses*. And this leads to my amazing publishers at Gallery Books and Simon & Schuster. The second I got on the phone with my editor, Natasha Simons, I just *knew* the stars had aligned. Just like Kendall and Brandi, you got me, you got *NLB*, you got everything. Thank you, Natasha and Hannah M. Brown, and everyone else who was patient AF when I had procrastinated like a monster.

Shout-out to Joe Weiner, my lawyer and friend, who has been forced to act as my manager year after year. You're a goddamn saint.

To my witches and my best girlfriends—the support y'all have shown me has made me feel so strong and safe. I don't want to get all "Live Laugh Love" on you (gross), but y'all have lifted me up when I've hit rock bottom and have grounded me when my bitchy Dark Passenger has been unleashed. There is nothing like a good girlfriend. You guys know who you are, and if you're still wondering, then you're probably not one of them.

Beau, I love you. You are the only man who has made me feel wholly comfortable and loved by being 100 percent myself. You have inspired me to write this book in so many ways, because you gave me the safe space to just be myself and write honestly. Also, I've never felt insecure watching a *Kardashian* marathon in front of you. That's *maje*.

To my delightful, intuitive, *genius* coconspirator, Dina Gachman. You're the mother freakin' wind beneath my wings. I must have done something right in one of my past lives, because I seeeeeeriously lucked out with you.

And finally to my Khaleesis: Thank you for laughing with me, crying with me, and judging with me. Connecting with all of you and having this little community has been one of the things I'm most proud of. You have given me purpose. And there is no greater gift than that. Well, maybe a diamond-encrusted ranch bottle, but you know.